GET YOUR BUNS IN HERE

Laurel A. Wicks

aka Bru

Originally printed as
Bru's Buns
&
Other High Altitude Delights
First Printing May 1981
Second Printing May 1982

Wimmer Brothers Printing 1985

10-Speed Publication 1987 & 1991

Illustrations by Stuart Auld,
with the exceptions of:
Whole Wheat & Light Rye
by Tom McMurray

Library of Congress Card Catalog 82-90437
ISBN 0-9606306-3-5

Printed by Grand Teton Lithography
Jackson, WY 83001

Laurel A. Wicks
Box 1470
Jackson, Wyoming
83001

Acknowledgements

There are many people to thank for this endeavor, beginning with my parents, whose lives reflect a vision and support that does not fail me. The generosity and encouragement of John Nooney, Alfred Ford, Ron Shapiro and Felix Buchenroth, Jr. made the bakery project possible. Blanche, a smart cookie and my left hand person, created some organization out of my chaos. The graphics are a product of the creative mind of Stuart Auld. Diane Kaup Benefiel guided the layout of the first printing. Maurice was there as an inspiration and proofreader. Individual recipe creations were developed by the people given credit at the top of the recipes. Employees, family, neighbors, customers and students have made up the fibers of my life and business. The dividing lines between those categories have become subtle or faded away entirely. Together they became the fabric of a bakery called Bru's Buns & Breads.

Laurel A. Wicks 1981

In 1980 I transformed the bakery into a restaurant called **The Bunnery**. It lives on, near the town square in Jackson, Wyoming. They still use many of these recipes and still sell the book. The changes and additions to this book reflect my life. I thank my wonderful friends and coworkers while living in New Orleans. I want to thank Joel Solomon and Martha Burton for their help keeping the book and my life moving forward, with a circle of support, many years ago during my Nashville incarnation. I acknowledge Phil Woods, 10-Speed Press, and Patti Breitman for their stewardship of the **Get your Buns in Here** book for many years. During another of my learning sojourns, I stumbled upon a little neighborhood on San Francisco Bay in California that was quite like home.
I'm grateful to all my pals at the very original Rosemary's Bakery in Point Richmond for sharing. Jeanne Robertson organized an index. For help and support on this revision I am grateful to David and Sherry O'Connor. Life is a series of grand adventures. I am grateful.

June 1999

To My Mother,
who presented me with a choice
when I was little,
"Would you like to weed the flower garden,
or make some cookies?"

Table of Contents

Chapter 6 BREADS & ROLLS

Chapter 7 CANDY

Chapter 8 CAKES & MUFFINS

Chapter 9 PIES & TARTS

Chapter 10 FROSTINGS, GLAZES, ICINGS & SAUCES

Index

Introduction

In the fall of 1974 a project began which consumed my life for many years. It began as a dream. It molded itself into a reality. A tiny log building which was originally built as a blacksmith shop, was transformed into a bakery. With borrowed money and some antique equipment local legend was born—Bru's Buns & Breads. This book contains most of the recipes and a few of the memories of that establishment.

The plan was to show the world that healthy foods were the ticket to happiness. My background in business was non-existent. A few home-sized recipes, all made with honey, instead of refined sugar, were the beginning. From this beginning evolved major changes in style. The first customers were welcomed on St. Patrick's Day 1975. "We want brownies, chocolate brownies!" "Cookies!" "Make us candy!" resounded the requests. The shock registered heavily. These people didn't want to hear my rap on health, and keeping the fans happy was a necessity. Since that day there have been many changes.

My product line was tempered for social compatibility and economic survival. I have learned to use sugar and chocolate as well as honey. I can cook for macrobiotics and omnivores, over campfires or in restaurants. My philosophy remains essentially the same. Eating is a vital part of our lives every day. The quality of the ingredients determines the outcome of the product. The foods that we consume literally become us. The materials our bodies and brains use to create are limited to what we feed ourselves. Bru's Buns & Breads always used the finest ingredients: real chocolate, extracts rather than imitation flavorings, high quality vegetable oils, butter, unbleached flour, whole grains, fresh fruits. I suggest that you do the same. I prefer foods organically grown and choose to support the people who grow foods organically. Be aware. Read labels. Choose mindfully.

The recipes in this book are a framework from which to learn. Experiment! Sometimes I follow these recipes just as they are written. Often I make substitutions. I leave out the nuts so I can share a treat with my brother who doesn't like nuts. Perhaps I discover that there are no lemons in my house, but lots of oranges. Be flexible. It helps.

Weather and mood effect baking. Low cloud ceilings slow down the rising process. Angry people's cakes fall. Bread dough loves to be pummeled. Baking is an excellent form of therapy.

The creative process can be extremely pleasurable. This book is for you. Have fun. Be tempted and create temptations. May the buns always rise.

Notes on the Recipes

These are some explanations to aid your baking adventures with this book.

- Read the whole recipe before you begin.

- Note the yield stated at the top of the recipe.

- The oven temperature is given at the top of the recipe. "Preheat" indicates that the recipe won't take long to make, so be sure to have the oven ready. When the recipe say "Bake at" it means that the procedures take longer, and somewhere in the directions it will tell you when to turn on the oven.

- Some recipes are fragile and timing is important. Pay attention to that, but don't be intimidated.

- It might be good to have pans ready as you start.

- Baking parchment paper is a wonderful thing. If you use it to line pans, the baked goods are less oily and clean up is easier.

- Butter isn't appropriate for pans, as it burns at a very low temperature. Vegetable oil works. Spray works, although the pump kind is perhaps better for the environment. Paper...trust me on this.

- Stainless steel is better in quality than aluminum in cooking and baking pans.

- To create a buttermilk or sour milk substitute, add a teaspoon of cider vinegar to a cup of milk and let it sit for a few minutes.

- Plain yogurt works as a healthful substitute for sour cream.

- The recipes use dried granulated yeast.

- Light brown cane sugar is what I mean by brown sugar.

- "c" stands for cup

- "t" stands for teaspoon

- "T" stands for tablespoon

• Some items, especially cookies continue to bake after they are taken from the oven. Taking them out of the oven a bit early helps to create a chewy texture.

• Test doneness by inserting a toothpick in the center of a cake or sweet bread.

• As my mom taught me, it is helpful to transfer cookies and glazed bread onto or over a cut up brown paper bag for cooling and oil absorption.

• Vegetable oils like soy or safflower are a healthy and reasonable substitute for butter. Use the same amount called for or even less if you have issues about calories from fats.

• I have set up this book with footers which say the name of the chapters. Within each chapter, the recipes are in alphabetical order. this makes it possible to flip through the book and find a recipe quite easily.

Notes on High Altitude Baking

These recipes were developed in Jackson Hole, Wyoming at an altitude of 6,200 feet. Much of what one reads or hears about high altitude baking is intimidating hype. Different conditions do exist at different altitudes, but the patterns are extremely logical.

There is less atmosphere above you pushing down. Cakes and breads rise more easily, therefore less leavening is needed. Decrease the amounts of baking soda, baking powder or yeast used in standard recipes.

The boiling temperature is lower, a phenomenon which effects baking results. Also, decrease the sweetener by a tablespoon per cup and increase the flour by the same amount.

Because the air is less dense at higher altitudes, it doesn't hold heat as well. It takes a bit more time to bake. Check your oven while things are baking.

Low altitude has its own set of circumstances. At sea level or below — don't laugh — the galley of a boat or the French Quarter in New Orleans are below sea level. You may need to increase the sweetening and the leavening or decrease the amount of flour. Baking time may decrease.

Doesn't all of this sound really easy and sensible? It is. Baking isn't a one time deal, it's an evolution. If you try a recipe and find the results less than perfect, make notes and try it again. Write in this book. Wear it out. Believe in yourself and be creative. Have fun.

If you have questions or requests, write them down and send them in my direction:

Bru's Buns
Box 1470
Jackson, Wyoming 83001

P.S. The illustrations throughout this book are available as postcards and may be purchased upon request.

BREAKFAST

Greetings from
BREADTAKING
ARCH OF BAGELS
GET YOUR BUNS IN HERE
WORLD FAMOUS SIGN
THE BIG BUN
SWAMI TOMMY
FRONT DOOR
HIPSTER
FRONT
COUNT
ZARDOZ
BREAD
LOAF-ING
GOD-
ZILLA
THE DUCHESS
AT WORK
SINKS
FRESH FRUIT
SWEET & BUNS
FLOUR SACKS
SKEENIK
TETONS
Jackson, Wyoming

As the Sheep Attack the Bakery Screaming Nonsense

Having sharpened the knife for the seventeenth time,
I see I've committed a sweetie bun crime.
In an effort to capture an absolute fluff
Was the tray barely pulled from the heat soon enough.
With all of my knowledge summoned up for this try
What have I created? Breakfast rolls, slightly dry.
Hopefully passing for a bit overdone,
They won't sit on the shelf being buncumbersome.
As I lesson-learned homeward the walk slowly trod,
Will I welcome my bed and the land ruled by nod.

Good morning, bru.

S. Doug Hettinger

What this earnest young employee lacked in skill, was supplemented by a different kind of inspiration. What a great guy. Wish he'd stop by.

— Bru 1999

Braided Cardamom Buns

Bake at 350°
Makes about 2 dozen

1 1/2 c warm water
1/2 c oil
1/2 c honey
2 1/2 T yeast
2 eggs
1 T ground cardamom
1 t salt
1/2 c powdered milk
6 c unbleached flour

milk
granulated sugar

In a large bowl combine the water, vegetable oil, and honey. Stir until the honey is mixed. Sprinkle in the yeast and stir until dissolved. When the yeast rises to the surface and begins to look foamy, add the eggs, cardamom, powdered milk and half of the flour. Beat at least one hundred strokes. Allow to rest for 10 minutes. Add the salt and the first cup of the remaining flour. Stir.

After the dough becomes too stiff to stir any longer, turn onto a lightly floured counter and knead about five minutes. Gradually add more flour until a soft but not sticky dough is achieved. Return to the bowl, and after lightly oiling the surface of the dough, cover and allow to rest until doubled.

Punch down and knead. Divide into two dozen pieces. Roll each into a coil about 7" long. Form each into a knot. Tuck both ends under. Place on a lightly oiled or papered tray.

Brush the rolls with milk and sprinkle with sugar. Allow to rise until doubled before placing in a heated 350° oven. Bake until browned, about 30 minutes. They may be cooled on a wire rack or on the papered pan.

Buttermilk Coffeecake

Russell Gilliam

Preheat oven to 350°
Makes 1 9" Round

1 1/2 c unbleached flour
1/3 c sugar
1/2 c brown sugar
1/2 t ground ginger
1 t cinnamon
3/8 c soft butter
1 egg
2/3 c buttermilk
1/2 t baking soda
1/2 t baking powder
1/2 t salt

1/2 c pecan pieces
2 t cinnamon

Measure into a mixing bowl the flour, sugars, ginger, cinnamon and salt. Stir until thoroughly mixed. Measure in the butter. Cut in with a pastry blender, or use a mixer to blend until mixed and crumbly.

Remove 2/3 cup of this mixture and transfer to a small bowl. Add the pecans and the 2 t cinnamon to this mixture and stir. Set aside.

Beat the egg into the batter in the mixing bowl. Gradually add the buttermilk, beating until the batter is light and smooth.

Sprinkle the baking soda and powder over the batter and mix until blended. Pour the batter into a 9" round pan that has been oiled and lined with parchment paper. Spread the batter evenly. Cover the top with the crumb mixture.

Place the coffeecake in an oven preheated to 350°. Baking time is about 25 minutes. Test carefully with a toothpick in the center to see if it is done. This cake can be quite delicate while baking, be careful.

Allow to cool at least 5 minutes before removing from pan. To accomplish this easily without losing topping, loosen the cake from the baking pan with a table knife. Place a large plate upside down on top of the cake. Turn it upside down. Remove paper. Place serving plate on top, invert and serve.

Danish Pastry

Bake at 400°
Makes about 3 dozen

8 c unbleached flour
1/2 c sugar
4 eggs at room temperature
1 1/2 c milk
1/2 c hot water
4 T yeast

1 1/4 lb butter

cinnamon
sugar
butter

Mix the flour and the sugar in a large mixing bowl. Break the eggs into a small bowl or cup, beat slightly with a fork. In a large measuring cup combine the milk, water and the yeast. Stir until the yeast is completely dissolved. It is important that the yeast does not become active. Pour the liquids into the dry mixture. Stir in. Add the eggs and mix until kneadable. Turn the dough onto a counter and knead until the dough becomes smooth and shiny. This seems to take almost forever.

Let the dough rest for at least 10 minutes in the refrigerator, well wrapped or covered in the bowl. Remove from the refrigerator and roll into a rectangular shape about 1/2 inch thick. Spread 2/3 of this rectangle with butter which is softened. Fold the unbuttered 1/3 toward the center, then the other third over this to create 5 layers, three layers of dough with the butter in between. Roll out again and repeat the procedure. Repeat for a third time to use up all of the butter.

Temperature is an important consideration. Keep the dough cool enough that the yeast doesn't start working or allow the butter to melt. Return the dough to the refrigerator, well wrapped, if it becomes too warm.

The rolling and folding process needs to be repeated three more times. On the last time that the dough is a large rectangle, spread the whole surface with a thin layer of softened butter. Cover 1/2 of this with a cinnamon sugar mix, then fold in half. Allow the dough to chill one more time.

Remove from the refrigerator and roll out to 1/2 inch thick. Cut into strips about 1/2 inch wide. Holding one end of the strip, roll the other end with your hand to make a spiral. Curl this around to make a flat coil. Tuck the outside end under. Place on a papered sheet.

Allow to rise until doubled in a place where it is not warm enough to melt the butter. Preheat the oven to 400 degrees. Place a spoonful of your favorite preserves in the center of each pastry before baking.

Bake until delicately golden. Glaze while still warm.

Granola

Shena Waugh Sandler

Preheat oven to 325°
Makes about 8 cups

4 c rolled oats
2/3 c sunflower seeds
1/3 c sesame seeds
2/3 c cashews
2/3 c almonds
2/3 c walnuts
1 c coconut
2/3 c vegetable oil
1 c honey
2 T vanilla extract
1/2 t salt
1/3 t ground cloves
2/3 t cinnamon

In a small saucepan combine the liquids and the spices. Heat, stirring occasionally to prevent burning. Do not allow to boil.

While the syrup is heating, mix the dry ingredients in a large bowl. Pour about a third of the syrup over the dry mix, stir to incorporate. Repeat until all is well mixed.

Spread on oiled or papered tray. Bake about twenty minutes or until golden. After about ten minutes, take the tray from the oven and stir, otherwise the corners get too done.

You may add dried fruits like raisins or currants.
Do this after the baked mixture has cooled.

Hot Crossed Buns

(But it's Lent)

Bake at 350°
Makes 2 dozen

2 1/2 c hot water
2/3 c honey
2 1/2 T yeast
1/4 c melted butter
2 eggs
2 oranges, juice & zest
1 c raisins
1 1/2 t cinnamon
1/2 t ground cloves
1/2 t nutmeg
1 c powdered milk
1 t salt
7 c unbleached flour

egg wash

Glaze with:
2 T water
1 1/2 T lemon juice
2 c powdered sugar

Break the eggs into a small bowl. Stir with a fork. Add the juice and zest of the oranges and set aside.

Pour the hot water into a mixing bowl and add the honey. Stir until dissolved. Sprinkle in the yeast and stir until dissolved. Allow to rest until the yeast just begins to foam.

Add half the flour and beat about 100 strokes until the dough is smooth and shiny. Let this rest for 10 minutes. Add the oranges, eggs, and melted butter. Stir. Add the spices, including the salt, the powdered milk and one cup of flour. Stir until evenly mixed. Gradually add more flour until a nice soft dough is formed. Knead on a lightly floured counter for about 5 minutes. Shape the dough into a ball, place it back in the mixing bowl, and lightly oil the surface. Let rise until doubled.

Punch down the dough and knead on a lightly floured counter for about 5 minutes. Let the dough rest while making an egg wash by breaking the egg into a cup and beating with about a tablespoon of water. Divide the dough into 2 dozen pieces. Shape into balls. Place on papered baking sheets. Brush the rolls with the egg wash.

Let rise until doubled, then place in a preheated 350 degree oven. Bake until golden. After they have cooled, glaze with crosses, either drizzled from a spoon or from a pastry bag.

Lately I have been making these with part whole wheat flour, some oat bran, egg whites instead of whole eggs, safflower oil instead of butter, no milk. The result is healthier and still very good.

Orange Currant Scones

Preheat oven to 400°
Makes about 2 dozen

4 1/2 c flour
3/4 c sugar
1 1/2 T baking powder
1 t salt
2 T orange zest
1 c currants
1 c butter or margarine
3 eggs
7/8 c milk or less

Mix all of the dry ingredients in a bowl. Cut in the butter or margarine. Beat the eggs in a separate bowl or a large liquid measuring cup. Add the milk to the eggs and stir again. Add the liquids to the dry. Toss with two forks to mix. Do not beat. Drop onto a papered baking sheet. Bake until golden.

One of the great things I have discovered about scones is that one may mix them up and bake as many as needed. Put the rest in the freezer, on a baking sheet. After they are frozen put them in a ziplock bag and bake them any time.

Poppy Seed Rolls

Rebecca Silva Stansberry

Bake at 350°
Makes 2 rolls

5-6 c unbleached flour
2 T yeast
1/3 c sugar
1 t salt
1 1/2 c milk
1/3 c vegetable oil
3 eggs

3/4 c poppy seeds
1 c boiling water
1/3 c honey
1/2 c chopped walnuts
1 T lemon zest
1 stiffly beaten egg white

In a large mixing bowl, combine the yeast with 2 cups of the sifted flour. Combine the milk, sugar, oil and salt in a saucepan and heat until warm, but not hot. Stir to prevent scorching. Add this to the dry ingredients. Add the eggs and beat until smooth, about 3 to 5 minutes. Add enough flour to make a moderately stiff dough. Turn onto a lightly floured counter, and knead until satiny, about 10 minutes. Shape into a ball. Return to the mixing bowl. Lightly oil the surface. Cover and let rise in a warm place until doubled. This will take about an hour.

While the dough is rising, make the poppy seed filling. Pour the cup of boiling water over the poppy seeds. Let stand for 30 minutes. Drain thoroughly. Grind the poppy seeds in a blender or food processor. Stir in the nuts, honey and lemon zest. Fold in the stiffly beaten egg white.

Punch down the dough. Divide the dough into halves. Cover and let rise for 10 minutes. On a lightly floured counter, roll one half of the dough into a rectangle about 20" x 8". Spread half of the filling evenly over the dough. Roll it up and seal the ends by tucking them under the roll. Place the roll seam side down in a 9" x 3" x 5" bread pan which is well oiled. Repeat this with the other half of the dough. Let rise until double.

Bake in a preheated oven for about 35 minutes or until nicely browned. Remove from the oven and allow to cool for 5 minutes before removing from the pans. Cool them on a wire rack.

Raisin Brioche

Rebecca Silva Stansberry

Bake at 350°
Makes 2 rings

1/2 c water
1 c scalded milk
1/3 c honey
1/4 c melted butter
2 T yeast
1 1/2 c raisins
3 eggs
1 t salt
5 1/2 c unbleached flour

1 egg yolk

Cover the raisins with boiling water and set aside. In a large mixing bowl combine the scalded milk, the water, and the honey. Stir until the honey is dissolved. Sprinkle in the yeast while continuing to stir. Let it rest until the yeast begins to foam. Add the raisins, well drained, the melted butter and the eggs. Stir in 3 cups of flour and beat well. Let rest for ten minutes.

Add the salt and the rest of the flour. Turn this soft dough onto a lightly floured surface and knead for 5 minutes. Place in the bowl and oil the surface. Cover and allow to rise until doubled.

Punch down the dough and knead lightly. Divide the dough in half and let it rest for ten minutes. Oil and flour 2 9" round baking pans. Shape each half of the dough into eight balls and place in the pans with a little space between each and the sides of the pans. With pastry scissors, cut an X in the top of each dough ball. Allow to rest until doubled.

Bake about 20 minutes. Remove the pans from the oven and brush the surfaces with an egg yolk beaten with 1 T water. Return to the oven and bake until golden.

Remove from the pans while still hot and cool on wire racks.

Rose's Danish

Rosemary Harbrecht

Bake at 375°
makes about 3 dozen

2 1/3 c bread flour
1 2/3 c pastry flour
2 1/2 T yeast
1/2 c sugar

4 eggs
2 t orange zest
water to make 2 cups

1 c softened butter

Filling:
8 oz cream cheese
1/4 c sugar
1 egg
1 t orange zest
1/2 c ricotta cheese

Stir the dry ingredients in a mixing bowl. Beat the eggs with the orange zest in a large measuring cup. Add enough cold water to make 2 cups. Add the wet ingredients to the dry and knead for a few minutes.

Roll the dough into a rectangle between 1/4 and 1/2 inch thick. Spread 1/2 cup of the softened butter on two thirds of the rectangle and fold the dough in thirds. Roll out to the same size again and spread the rest of the butter and fold again. Roll and fold again.

Wrap the dough double thick in plastic wrap and refrigerate overnight.

To make the filling, combine all of the ingredients in a food processor and mix until smooth. The filling will keep well if refrigerated.

Roll the dough into a large rectangle and cut into 5 inch squares. Spoon some cheese filling into the middle of each square and fold in the corners, all four or two diagonal. Place on a papered baking sheet. Let them rest for about 10 minutes before baking until golden.

Scones Rosita

Rosemary Harbrecht

Preheat oven to 400°
Makes about 2 dozen

4 1/2 c flour
1 1/3 T baking powder
1 c brown sugar
1 t salt
1/2 t nutmeg
2/3 c raisins or dried cranberries
3/4 c butter or margarine
3 eggs
1 c buttermilk

cinnamon sugar

Mix the dry ingredients in a bowl. Cut in the butter or margarine. In a separate bowl beat the eggs, then add the buttermilk and beat a bit more. Add to the dry ingredients and mix, but do not overmix. Cut or drop into shapes on a papered pan. Sprinkle with cinnamon sugar. Bake until golden, about 20 minutes.

Sweet E. Buns

Barbara Sanford Smith

Bake at 325°
Makes 2 9" rings

2 c milk
1/4 c honey
2 T yeast
1/4 c melted butter
1 t salt
4 1/2 c unbleached flour

melted butter
brown sugar
cinnamon
fruits & nuts

Warm the milk and honey. Pour into a mixing bowl and sprinkle in the yeast, stirring until dissolved. Allow this to rest until the yeast rises to the surface and starts to become foamy. Pour in the butter and about half the flour. Beat until the dough becomes smooth and shiny. Allow the dough to rise for 10 minutes. Add the salt and one more cup of flour. Stir until smooth. Add more flour until it is hard to stir. Turn onto a lightly floured counter and knead gently, adding more flour but making sure the dough remains very soft.

Allow to rise again for 10 to 15 minutes. While the dough is rising, prepare the melted butter and the fillings of your choice. Bananas and walnuts are dynamite. Apples and raisins have their appeal. Oil and flour the pans and set aside.

Punch down the dough and turn onto a floured counter. Shape into a rectangle, then roll out until the dough is about 8 inches from front to back, 1/4 inch thick and about 20 inches long. Brush the dough with melted butter. Sprinkle with an even cover of brown sugar. Dust with cinnamon (and a trace of cloves or nutmeg, perhaps). Roll into a 20 inch loaf. Slice off pieces about 1 inch thick. Place half in each of the pans. Allow to rest on top of the oven or some warm place while the oven preheats.

Bake for about 30 minutes or until the buns are nicely browned. Cover with a thin coating of glaze while they are still warm. After they have cooled, use the rest of the glaze to make a striped pattern on the buns.

COOKIES

Almond Cookies

Preheat oven to 300°
Makes 3 dozen

1 1/4 c sugar
1 1/4 c butter
2 eggs
1 t almond extract
1/2 t lemon extract
1/2 t salt
1 t baking powder
3 c unbleached flour

whole or slivered almonds

Thoroughly cream the butter and sugar. Add the eggs and beat until light in color. Add the extracts and the salt. Add the baking powder with the first cup of flour, and stir well. Gradually add the rest of the flour until the dough is firm, but not dry.

Shape into 1" balls. Place on a papered tray and flatten. Press one whole almond or many slivers of almond in the top of each cookie.

Bake for about 15 minutes, until they barely start to brown. Allow to cool at least 5 minutes on the tray before removing.

Chewy Oatmeal Cookies

Preheat oven to 350°
Makes about 5 dozen

1 1/4 c butter
1 c brown sugar
1 c sugar
2 eggs
1 t vanilla extract
1/2 t salt
1 t nutmeg
1 t cinnamon
1 c coconut
2 1/2 c rolled oats
1 t baking soda
1 1/2 c unbleached flour

Thoroughly cream the butter and sugars. Whip in the eggs until light. Add the vanilla, salt and spices, then the coconut. Stir. Add the rolled oats and stir thoroughly. You may let the dough rest for a few minutes before adding the flour. This allows quite a bit of moisture to be absorbed by the coconut and oats. Add the flour and the baking soda. The dough will be a bit sticky.

Roll into one inch balls or drop onto a papered baking sheet. Bake until lightly golden, about 12 minutes.

Chocolate Chip Cookies

(Corrected at last!)

Preheat oven to 350°
Makes about 5 dozen

- 1 1/2 c vegetable oil
- 1 1/8 c sugar
- 1 1/8 c brown sugar
- 3 eggs
- 1 1/2 t baking soda
- 1 t salt
- 1 1/2 t vanilla extract
- 3 3/8 c unbleached flour
- 12 oz chocolate chips

Thoroughly cream the oil and the sugars. Add the eggs and beat until light. Mix in the salt and vanilla. Add the flour a cup at a time, stirring in after each addition. Add the baking soda with the second or third cup of flour. Stir in the chocolate chips.

This dough will be quite sticky, which makes for chewy cookies, but a bit harder to handle. Flour your hands lightly to keep the dough from sticking if you want to form 1" balls of dough to make the cookies round. You may want to use a spoon to drop the cookies onto papered sheets. Bake until lightly golden, about 12 minutes.

Another way to keep cookies chewy is to make sure you take them from the oven while they are still soft.

(For years the line of type which was: 1 1/8 c brown sugar has been missing from the book. This is regrettable and I am sorry.)

Chocolate Peanut Butter Pinwheels

Mom aka Peg Donaldson

Bake at 350°
Makes about 3 dozen

1 c vegetable oil
2 c sugar
1 c peanut butter
2 eggs
4 T milk
2 1/2 c unbleached flour
1 t baking soda
1/2 t salt
2 c melted chocolate chips

Cream the vegetable oil and sugar. Add the peanut butter (I use the kind that has no additives), the eggs and the milk. Stir well. Add the flour, the salt and the baking soda, and stir until completely blended.

Divide the dough in half. On a sheet of waxed paper, roll out half the dough into a rectangle 8" x 15" x 1/4". Spread half of the melted chocolate evenly over the rectangle. Roll up to form a log 15" long and 2" in diameter. Wrap well and refrigerate. Do the same procedures with the other half.

The dough needs to be refrigerated for at least 30 minutes. Preheat the oven to 350°. Slice the rolls into cookies about 1/3 inch thick. Bake on papered trays or ungreased sheets for about 8 to10 minutes.

Yummo! These are the best in years. We make them for holidays, and invent as many holidays as we can.

Cut Out Cookies

Jeanne Midnight

Bake at 325°
Makes about 3 dozen

- 1 c butter
- 1 c sugar
- 2 eggs
- 1 t baking soda
- 2 t cream of tartar
- 1/2 t salt
- 1 t vanilla extract
- 3 c unbleached flour

Thoroughly cream the butter and the sugar. Add the eggs and whip until light. Stir in the vanilla. Sift the flour and add to it the baking soda, the cream of tartar and the salt. Sift the dry ingredients into the batter, gradually blending it in. The dough will be sticky. Form a rectangle with the dough before you refrigerate it, which will be easier to roll it out. Make sure the dough is well chilled before you roll it out.

Preheat the oven to 325°. Roll on a well floured surface. Flour the surface of the dough to make sure the rolling pin doesn't stick. Dipping the cookie cutters in flour also helps. Transfer the cookies to a papered tray to bake. Remove the cookies from the oven before they start to brown, which is about 10 minutes or less.

Frost the cookies after they are thoroughly cooled.

Ginger Crinkles

Janet McPherson Wershow

Preheat oven to 350°
Makes about 5 dozen

1 1/2 c vegetable oil
2 c sugar
2 eggs
1/2 c molasses
1 T baking soda
1 t salt
2 t cinnamon
1 t ground cloves
2 t ginger
4 1/2 c unbleached flour

granulated sugar

Thoroughly cream the oil and the sugar. Add the eggs and beat until light. Add the molasses and blend in. Add the spices and stir. Add the baking soda while adding the flour, cup by cup.

Shape the cookies into 1" balls. Roll the cookies in granulated sugar. Bake on papered trays for about 12 minutes.

Half Moons
Sour Cream Cookies

Catherine Woods / Grandma Jones

Preheat oven to 375°
Makes about 3 dozen

2 eggs
1 c sugar
1/2 c sour cream
1/3 c softened butter
2 c unbleached flour
1/2 t baking soda

Catherine's version:
chocolate and
vanilla icing

Grandma's version:
1 t nutmeg
raisins
granulated sugar

Beat the eggs thoroughly. Add the sugar, the sour cream and the softened butter. Whip until light. Add the flour and the baking soda. Drop by the spoonful onto papered trays. Bake until they spring back, but do not let them brown.

To create Catherine's Half Moons:
After the cookies have cooled, frost half of each cookie with chocolate icing and the other half with vanilla.

To create Grandma's Sour Cream Cookies:
Add the teaspoon of nutmeg to the batter and turn onto a lightly floured counter. Gently roll the dough to about 3/8 inch thick and cut with a round, scalloped edged cutter. Transfer with a spatula to a papered try and place a raisin in the center of each. Sprinkle with granulated sugar before baking.

Healthier Oatmeal Cookies

Preheat oven to 350°
Makes about 5 dozen

3/4 c vegetable oil
3/4 c brown sugar
2 ripe bananas
4 egg whites
1 t vanilla extract
1 t nutmeg
1 t cinnamon
3 c rolled oats
1 1/2 t baking soda
1 3/4 c whole wheat flour

These cookies evolved for a cooking class at the Senior Center of Jackson Hole. I'm always looking for healthier versions of treats and my pals at the Senior Center are always willing to eat them.

Thoroughly mix the vegetable oil and the brown sugar. Add the bananas, and mash them really well with a fork. Beat them into the batter. Add the egg whites and beat well. Stir in the spices, and then the oats. Add the baking soda with the flour and stir well.

Drop onto papered sheets and bake in the preheated oven for about 10 to 12 minutes.

Orange Cookies

David Samualson's Aunt Edith

Preheat oven to 350°
Makes about 4 dozen

1 1/2 c sugar
1 c softened butter
3 eggs
1 t salt
1 c sour cream
Juice and zest from one orange
1 t baking soda
1 t baking powder
3 3/4 c unbleached flour

Cream the butter and the sugar thoroughly. Add the eggs and beat until light. Add the salt, sour cream and the orange. Add one cup of the flour and stir all of these. Stir the baking soda and baking powder into the flour as you add the flour. The batter will be quite moist.

Drop by spoonfuls onto papered sheets. Bake in the preheated oven for about 10 minutes. The cookies will spring back to a light touch, but will not be browned.

After they have cooled you may frost the bottoms with orange icing.

Peanut Butter Cookies

Preheat oven to 350°
Makes about 3 dozen

2/3 c vegetable oil
1 c peanut butter
1 c sugar
1 1/4 c brown sugar
3 eggs
1 t vanilla extract
1/2 t salt
1 1/2 t baking powder
1 t baking soda
2 3/4 c unbleached flour

Cream the vegetable oil, peanut butter, and both kinds of sugar. Add the eggs and beat until light. Mix in the vanilla. Add the rising agents with the first cup of flour. The dough should not be dry.

Shape into 1" balls. Flatten slightly on the papered baking sheet. Make an X with the tines of a fork on each cookie before baking. Bake about 10 to 12 minutes.

Pecan Nougats

Mom aka Peg Donaldson

Preheat oven to 350°
Makes about 4 dozen

1 c softened butter
1/4 c sugar
1/2 t vanilla extract
1/2 t salt
2 c finely chopped pecans
1 3/4 c unbleached flour

powdered sugar

Thoroughly cream the butter and sugar. Add the vanilla and stir. In a separate bowl mix the flour, pecans and the salt. Gradually incorporate the dry ingredients until you have a smooth dough.

Shape into 1" balls. Place on papered sheets and bake about 10 minutes.

These cookies are very delicate. They break easily, which means that you will have to eat them. Be careful! Roll the cookies in powdered sugar once while they are still slightly warm and again after they have cooled.

Refrigerator Cookies

Mom's Recipe or Not,
Depending on How You Look at It

Bake at 400°
Makes about 3 dozen

The REAL Recipe:
1/2 c shortening
1/2 c brown sugar
3/4 c sugar
1 egg
1 t vanilla extract
1/2 c nut meats
2 c flour
1/2 t salt
2 t baking powder

What I thought:
1/2 c butter
1 c brown sugar
2 eggs
1/2 t cream of tartar
1/2 t salt
1 t baking soda
1 t vanilla extract
3/4 c chopped pecans
2 c unbleached flour

There was a mix up with this old family recipe which took me years to figure out. The real secret is to use wild hickory nuts. I wish you the best of luck finding them. If you have a chance, plant a tree. The other noteworthy aspect is that my mom always says "nut meats".

Cream the butter (or shortening) and the sugar (or sugars.) Beat thoroughly. Add the egg (or eggs) and beat until light. Blend in the spices. Stir in the nuts. Add the flour and stir until thoroughly mixed.

Shape into a roll, wrap in waxed paper, and refrigerate until thoroughly chilled. Preheat the oven to 400°. Slice the roll into pieces about 1/3 inch thick. Place on a papered tray and bake until lightly browned.

Scottish Shortbread

Shena's Granny

Preheat oven to 325°
Makes about 3 dozen

1 c butter
3/4 c sugar
2 1/4 c unbleached flour

Thoroughly cream the butter and sugar. This is easier if the butter is slightly soft. Stir in the flour. Knead the dough for 10 to 15 minutes. This makes the shortbread very tender.

Roll the dough on a lightly floured counter until it is about 3/8 inch thick. Cut the dough into "fingers" about 3/4 inch by 3 or 4 inches. Transfer the shortbread to a papered tray. Make a pattern of holes along the shortbreads. Holding the fork in a flat position, make a mark at each end about 1/3 inch long. Bake until golden.

Sesame Cookies

Preheat oven to 350°
Makes about 3 dozen

3/4 c vegetable oil
1 c brown sugar
1 egg
1 t vanilla extract
1/2 t baking soda
1 t baking powder
1/2 t salt
1/2 c coconut
1 c sesame seeds
2 c unbleached flour

Most people just go for the old standard cookie recipes. These are really delicious. Try them, you'll like them.

Toast the sesame seeds and the coconut on a clean dry pan. Stir occasionally and don't let them burn.

Thoroughly cream the vegetable oil and the brown sugar. Add the egg and beat until light in color. Add the vanilla, salt, baking soda and baking powder. Stir in the toasted ingredients. Add the flour one cup at a time and stir. The dough will be moist but not sticky. Roll into 1" balls and bake on papered trays until they are golden, which will be about 10 minutes.

Shelly's Chocolate Fantasies

Inspired by Shelly Shapiro

Preheat oven to 350°
Makes about 5 dozen

- 1 1/4 c vegetable oil
- 1 1/2 c sugar
- 1 3/4 c brown sugar
- 3 eggs
- 1/2 t salt
- 2 t baking soda
- 1 c cocoa
- 1 c walnuts
- 2 t vanilla extract
- 3 3/4 c unbleached flour

Thoroughly cream the oil and the sugars. Add the eggs and beat until light, at least 5 minutes. Add the salt, cocoa, walnuts and vanilla. Measure in the baking soda with the first cup of flour and stir. Add the flour cup by cup, stirring after each addition. The dough should be moist but not sticky.

Shape into 1" balls. Roll in powdered sugar and place on papered trays. Bake about 10 minutes, making sure to remove them from the oven before they get dry.

Snickerdoodles

The cookies that make you laugh
Catherine Gwendolyn

Preheat oven to 375°
Makes about 4 dozen

1 c vegetable oil
2 eggs
1 1/2 c sugar
2 t cream of tartar
1 t baking soda
1/4 t salt
2 2/3 c unbleached flour
1/2 c raisins

cinnamon
granulated sugar

Thoroughly cream the oil and the sugar. Add the eggs and beat until light. Measure in the cream of tartar, salt and baking soda and stir into batter. Add the flour a cup at a time, stirring after each addition. Add the raisins and stir them in evenly.

Shape the dough into 1" balls. Roll them in a cinnamon sugar mix that is about equal volumes of each.

Press them onto papered trays. Bake about 10 minutes, until they are a bit soft in the centers.

Snow Flurries

Rosemary Harbrecht

Bake at 350°
Makes 6-7 dozen

- 1 1/2 c sugar
- 1 1/3 T lemon zest
- 7/8 cup butter
- 2/3 c shortening
- 3 eggs
- 1 t vanilla extract
- 1/2 t almond extract
- 1/2 t salt
- 1/2 t baking powder
- 4 1/2 c unbleached flour

These are my latest favorite holiday roll out cookies. They are tasty and very tender.

Thoroughly cream the sugar, the butter, the shortening and the lemon zest. Add the eggs, one at a time, and stir. Beat the batter until it becomes light. Add the almond and vanilla extracts, and stir. Mix in the salt and the baking powder with the first cup of flour. Add the rest of the flour one cup at a time, stirring after each addition.

Shape the dough into two rectangular shapes, and wrap in plastic wrap. Chill well before rolling.

Roll out on a floured counter. Cut with floured cutters. Transfer to papered trays with a metal spatula. Bake for about ten minutes, until they barely start to brown.

Soft Molasses

Grandma Jones

Preheat oven to 350°
Makes about 30 cookies

3/4 c softened butter
1/4 c brown sugar
1/2 c molasses
1/2 c buttermilk
1/4 t salt
1/2 t cinnamon
1 t baking soda
1 3/4 c unbleached flour

Combine the softened butter and the brown sugar. Mix until smooth. Add the molasses and stir until smooth. Stir in the buttermilk until the mixture is evenly blended.

In a separate bowl, mix the salt, cinnamon and baking soda into the flour. Gradually mix the dry ingredients into the batter.

Drop from an oiled spoon onto papered trays. Bake 8-10 minutes, until they bounce back from a soft-fingered touch.

Thumbprints

Mom aka Peg Donaldson

Preheat oven to 350°
Makes about 3 dozen

1 c butter
1/2 c sugar
3 egg yolks
1 t vanilla extract
2 c unbleached flour
1/2 t salt

pecan halves
candies
raspberry preserves

Thoroughly cream the butter and the sugar. Stir in the egg yolks, one at a time, then add the vanilla and thoroughly beat. Blend in the salt and the flour. Refrigerate the dough for an hour. Roll into 1" balls. Place on a papered tray. Make a thumbprint impression in each cookie. Fill with a nut or a candy or preserves.

Bake for about 10 minutes, until delicately golden.

DESSERTS & PASTRIES

Baklava

A learning inspired by Timothy Hart Fennell

Preheat oven to 300°
Makes a 9" x 13" pan

1 lb phyllo dough
3/4 c butter
3 c finely chopped nuts

SYRUP:
3 c water
2 1/2 c honey
1 T lemon juice
1 t finely grated lemon peel
6 whole cloves
1 stick cinnamon
1 star anise

Melt the butter. After letting it sit undisturbed for a few minutes, clarify it by first skimming off the foamy surface. Next, separate the clear yellow liquid from the milky white liquid in the bottom. Retain and use the clarified butter.

Using a pastry brush, cover the bottom and sides of the pan with butter. Open the phyllo and place one paper thin leaf in the bottom of the pan. Butter the surface of the phyllo. If the phyllo is larger than the pan, then fold it over on top the buttered surface and butter again. Add another sheet of phyllo and butter again. Repeat until about 1/4 of the phyllo has been used. Spread 1 cup of the nuts evenly over the dough. Continue with the phyllo, butter repetitions until 1/2 the phyllo is used. Add another cup of nuts. Use the last cup of nuts after about 3/4 of the phyllo layers are used. With a very sharp knife cut the baklava into diamond shapes.

Place the pan in the preheated oven and turn down the heat to 250°. Baking time is about 2 hours. The pastry will rise and become lightly golden.

To make the syrup: Combine all of the ingredients in a saucepan. Bring to a boil, then reduce heat to a simmer. Reduce until the texture is syrupy while the pastry is baking. Remove the spices before using.

Take the baklava from the oven and pour 1/2 the syrup evenly over the pastry. Return to the oven for 10 minutes. Add the rest of the syrup and return to the oven for 5 more minutes.

Traditionally walnuts are used and sugar in the syrup. I use a combination of cashews, almonds and pecans and honey in the syrup.

Blue Cheese Cake

with Cognac Sauce
for Roy Guste, Jr.

Preheat oven to 375°
Makes one 10" cake

Crust:
1 1/2 c graham crackers
1/2 c unbleached flour
1/3 c sugar
1 t cinnamon
1/2 c softened butter
2 egg yolks

Filling:
20 oz cream cheese
5 oz blue cheese
1 c sour cream
1/3 c cream
2/3 c sugar
4 eggs
1 T cognac or brandy
1 t vanilla extract

Sauce:
2 lb seedless grapes
1 c water
1/2 c honey
1 c sugar
juice of 1 lemon
1/4 cognac or brandy

To make the crust: Combine the dry ingredients in a bowl. Blend in the softened butter. Add the egg yolks and stir until a moldable dough is formed. Press about a third of the crust mix into the bottom of a springform pan and bake for about 10 minutes. Remove from the oven and allow to cool. Press the remaining crust mix onto the sides of the pan and set aside. Lower the oven temperature to 250°.

To make the filling: Whip the cream cheese until soft. Crumble the blue cheese into the bowl and whip until the lumps disappear. Add the sour cream, the cream, and the sugar and beat until smooth. Add the eggs, one at a time, beating after each addition. Last, add the vanilla and the cognac and stir. Pour the filling mix into the springform pan and bake. Bake about 1 1/2 hours. The cake will puff but should not crack or turn brown.

Allow to cool to room temperature before refrigerating. Refrigerate at least a day before removing the springform and serving.

To make the sauce: Wash the grapes and remove all of the stems. Mash the grapes or partially puree in a blender or food processor. Combine all of the ingredients except the cognac, in a saucepan, bring to a boil, then reduce heat to simmer. Allow to reduce until a thick sauce consistency is achieved. Remove from heat and stir in the cognac. Pour over the top of the cheesecake before serving.

Bread Pudding

with Rum Sauce

Preheat oven to 325°
Makes 8 servings

Pudding:
6 c cubed stale bread
2 t baking soda
1/2 c raisins
2 eggs
3/4 c milk or cream
1 t vanilla extract
1/2 t nutmeg
1/4 c pineapple juice
1/4 c rum

Rum Sauce:
3/4 c brown sugar
1/4 c honey
3/8 c butter
2 T rum
1 T Gran Marnier
1 t vanilla extract
1 c crushed pineapple

To make the pudding: Whole grain breads will work, although traditionally this is made with white bread. Preheat the oven and place a pan of water on the lower rack. Put the cubed bread in a bowl and sprinkle the baking soda over the cubes. Toss. Blend in the raisins.

In a different mixing bowl, beat the eggs well. Add all of the other ingredients and beat well. Pour the liquids over the dry ingredients. Stir. Allow to sit for several minutes to absorb the liquids.

Spray well 8 individual molds or one large one.
Put the mix, divided equally into the individual molds or the large one. Bake on the upper rack in the oven, about 35 minutes for individual molds or 45 to 50 minutes for the large one. Allow to cool before removing from molds.

To make the sauce: Melt the butter in a sauce pan. Stir in the brown sugar. Add the honey and stir. Remove from the heat and stir in the remaining ingredients. Simmer until a sauce-like quality is achieved. Spoon over the pudding and serve while the sauce is hot.

Cannoli

(or as we call them: Knowles)
Enza Macri

Makes about 18 pastries

This recipe is so delicious that I included it, even though the shells are deep fried. Not the healthiest way to cook, but worthwhile as an exception. Read the whole recipe before beginning.

Filling:
3 c ricotta
1 1/4 c sugar
2 t vanilla extract
optional: 1/4 c grated semi-sweet chocolate

Shells:
3 c unbleached flour
1/4 c sugar
1 t cinnamon
1/4 t salt
3 T butter
2 eggs
2 T vinegar
2 T water

egg wash

finely chopped pistachios
powdered sugar

To make the filling: Combine the ricotta, sugar and vanilla. Beat until smooth. The grated chocolate may be folded into the mix, if you wish.

To make the shells: Combine the dry ingredients in a bowl. With a fork or pastry blender, cut in the butter until a pebbly texture is achieved. Mix the eggs into the liquids and add 1 spoonful at a time. Turn the dough onto a lightly floured counter and knead for 5 minutes. Wrap the dough well and refrigerate until thoroughly chilled.

In a deep pan or deep fryer, heat vegetable oil to 360°.

Make an oval pattern from cardboard or roll the cannoli dough into ovals about 6" x 4 1/2" by 1/8" thick. Before placing in the frying oil, wrap the shells around dowels 6" long and 1" in diameter. Fry until golden. Cool on paper towels to absorb excess oil. Remove the dowels while still warm.

Cool the shells completely before filling. After they are filled, dip the ends in the pistachios. Dust the tops with powdered sugar.

Cheesecake Brujaja

Preheat oven to 375°
Makes 1 10" cake

Crust:
1/3 c sugar
1 1/2 c unbleached flour
1 1/2 t lemon zest
1/4 t cinnamon
1/4 t ginger
2/3 c butter
2 egg yolks
1 t molasses
1/2 t vanilla extract

Filling:
32 oz cream cheese
2/3 c sour cream
1 1/3 c sugar
4 eggs
2 egg yolks
2 T unbleached flour
1/4 t salt
3/4 t lemon zest
1 t vanilla extract

To make the crust: Combine the dry ingredients in a bowl. Blend in the softened butter. Stir the beaten egg yolks with the molasses and the vanilla then add to the crust mix. Blend in thoroughly.

Press half of the crust mix into the bottom of a 10" springform pan. Bake about 10 minutes. After it has cooled, press the remainder around the side of the pan.

To make the filling: Beat the cream cheese until soft. Add the sour cream and the sugar and beat well. Add the eggs and the egg yolks and beat well again. Stir in the vanilla, lemon zest, flour and salt. Pour into the pan and place in the oven. Reduce the temperature to 250°. Bake for more than an hour, until the cake is set to the center. Do not let it crack or brown.

Cool it to room temperature before refrigerating. Let it set for a day before removing the springform or serving.

Chocolate Eclairs

In memory of Jug Bacon

Preheat oven to 400°
Makes about 18 pastries

Custard:
2/3 c sugar
6 T cornstarch
1/2 t salt
6 egg yolks
3 c milk
1 1/2 t vanilla extract
4 T butter
1 c whipping cream

Shells:
1 c water
1/4 c butter
1/8 t salt
1 c flour
5 eggs, room temperature

Glaze:
1/4 c cocoa
1/2 c water
1 t vanilla extract
powdered sugar

To make the custard: Measure the dry ingredients into the top of a double boiler or a stainless steel bowl that sits over a saucepan. Whisk in the milk a cup at a time, making sure there are no lumps. Add the vanilla and stir. Place the bowl over the saucepan which is half full of water. Cook, whisking occasionally until the custard is very thick. Add the butter and stir after it has melted. Cover with plastic wrap after it has cooled to room temperature and refrigerate. Just before you fill the shells, whip the cream and fold into the custard mix.

To make the shells: Bring the water and the butter to a boil in a saucepan. In a mixing bowl combine the flour and the salt. When the water has boiled, add to the dry ingredients all at once. Stir, then add the eggs one at a time and beat after each addition. Spoon or use a pastry tube with a huge plain tip to pipe the batter into 5 inch strips onto a papered sheet. Bake about 30 minutes or until the shells are puffy and browned.

After the shells have cooled, slit the tops and remove the pulp inside. Pipe in the custard mix and chill.

To make the glaze: Stir the water into the cocoa. Add the vanilla. Add powdered sugar to create a consistency which can be brushed onto the eclairs with a pastry brush.

Chocolate Soufflé

Preheat oven to 400°
Makes 4 servings

3 T butter
6 eggs
1/4 t salt
3 T unbleached flour
1 1/4 c unsweetened chocolate
4 T light rum
2 t vanilla extract
6 T sugar

butter
sugar
whipping cream

Prepare an 8" soufflé dish by adding a collar made of parchment paper which is pinned with a toothpick at the overlap and tied on with string. Butter the inside of the collar and the dish with softened butter and dust with sugar.

Separate the eggs, putting the whites in a bowl large enough to whisk until stiff. Set the yolks aside in a measuring cup. Before whisking the egg whites, scald the milk and set aside. Melt the butter in a saucepan over low heat. Add the flour and stir until smooth. Add the milk gradually and stir over low heat until thickened. Add the chocolate and stir until the chocolate has melted. Remove from the heat and add the egg yolks a bit at a time until all are added. Return to the heat and stir until thickened. Remove from the heat and stir in the sugar, salt, vanilla and the rum. Set this mix aside while you whisk the egg white until stiff, but not dry. Fold about 1/4 of the sauce mix into the whites, then repeat until all of the sauce is folded into the whites. Gently transfer the mixture into the soufflé dish.

Place the soufflé dish in the preheated oven and lower the temperature to 375°. Do not disturb for 30 minutes. Beat the cream and flavor with vanilla or rum and powdered sugar. After removing the soufflé from the oven, remove the collar and serve with the whipped cream (while still hot).

High Tea Scones

Preheat oven to 400°
Makes about 3 dozen

3 1/2 c unbleached flour
1 1/2 T baking powder
1/3 c sugar
1 t salt
2/3 c butter
2/3 c cream
4 eggs

egg wash
powdered sugar

Sift the dry ingredients into a mixing bowl. Cut the butter into this until pebbly and well blended. Form a well in the center. In a small bowl beat the eggs, then add the cream and beat again. Pour this mix into the well in the dough. Mix together by tossing with two forks until mixed. Do not overbeat.

Pat the dough gently onto a lightly floured counter until the dough is about 1/2 inch thick. Cut with cookie cutters or with a knife into diamond shapes. Transfer with a metal spatula onto a papered tray. Brush with the egg wash and sprinkle with powdered sugar.

Place the tray in the oven and reduce heat to 375°. Bake 12 to 15 minutes or until golden.

Lemon Sponge Pudding

Mom aka Peg Donaldson

Preheat oven to 325°
Serves 4 delicately

3 eggs
3/4 c sugar
3 T unbleached flour
3 T lemon juice
2 T orange juice
3 T lemon zest
2 T orange zest
1/8 t salt

whipped cream

Prepare and set aside the citrus juices and zest. Separate the eggs. In a small mixing bowl, beat the yolks with the sugar until it is light. Alternately add the flour and the citrus until all are evenly blended. Stir in the salt.

Beat the egg whites until stiff. Gently fold the lemon mix into the egg whites, a bit at a time. Carefully transfer the pudding mix to a buttered glass baking dish. Set the glass dish in a pan of hot water. Place in the preheated oven and bake for about 30 minutes. The pudding will be lightly golden on top.

Allow to cool to room temperature, then chill well before serving. Whip the cream and flavor with vanilla and powdered sugar.

My mom served this on very special occasions in stemmed glasses when we were kids.

Linzertorte

Bart Shoemaker

Bake at 325°
Makes 1 9" tart

2/3 c hazelnuts
1 c butter
3/4 c sugar
1/2 t vanilla extract
1 1/2 c unbleached flour
1 T cinnamon
1 t baking powder
1 c raspberry preserves

powdered sugar

Roast the hazelnuts in a dry pan in the oven for about 10 minutes. Wrap them in a clean dry towel after they come out of the oven. After they have cooled, roll them in the towel to remove the skins.

Puree the hazelnuts in a food processor with the sugar. Add the butter and the vanilla and mix until smooth. Add the flour with the baking powder and cinnamon. Pulse until evenly mixed.

Press about 2/3 of the dough into the tart pan. Roll the remainder of the dough or pat it into a rectangle about 9" long on a papered pan. Cut it into strips and then put the tray and the shell in the freezer. This is the best thing that I've figured out. The dough is too soft to move, but after it is frozen, the strips are handled easily.

Preheat the oven and remove the tart pieces from the freezer. Fill the shell with raspberry preserves and lay the strips over the top in a lattice pattern. Bake about 35 minutes. The preserves will be bubbling to the center and the crust will be lightly browned.

Allow to cool before removing from pan. You might dust lightly with powdered sugar before serving.

Too Chocolate Chocolate

Preheat oven to 375°
Makes 1 10" pie

Crust:
2 c graham cracker crumbs
2/3 c unbleached flour
1/4 c cocoa
1/2 c sugar
1/2 c butter
2 egg yolks

Filling:
16 oz cream cheese
2/3 c sugar
3 eggs
2/3 c cream
1 T triple sec
2 T creme de cacao
1 t vanilla extract
1/4 c cocoa

Mousse:
3 egg whites at room temperature
1 1/2 c cream
1 T creme de cacao
1 t vanilla extract
3 T cocoa
1/2 c sugar

whipped cream
chocolate shavings

To make the crust: Combine the graham cracker crumbs, flour, sugar and cocoa in a bowl. Cut the softened butter into this. Add the egg yolks to the mix and stir until a soft dough is formed. Press the dough into a 10" pie pan. Perforate with a fork in several places. Bake for 10 minutes in the preheated oven. Remove from the oven and set aside. Reduce the oven temperature to 250°.

To make the filling: Whip the cream cheese until it is soft and smooth. Add the sugar and beat until smooth. Add the eggs, one at a time, beating after each addition. Sprinkle in the cocoa while beating very slowly. Make sure all of the lumps are gone. Add the cream, triple sec, creme de cacao, and the vanilla. Pour into the crust and bake until set to the center, about an hour. Allow to cool to room temperature before refrigerating.

To make the mousse: Add the sugar to the egg whites. Whip until the mixture is stiff and shiny. Set aside. Whip the cream until it forms peaks. Sift the cocoa onto the surface, a bit at a time and fold in. Add the creme de cacao and the vanilla. Fold in. Fold the egg whites into the cream.

After the filling has completely chilled, score some marks on the surface of the filling. Add the mousse on top of the filling. Chill.

Serve with whipped cream and chocolate shavings.

SQUARES & BARS

Birdfood Bars

Preheat oven to 350°
Makes 2 dozen

1 1/4 c honey
1/2 c peanut butter
1 1/2 t vanilla
1/4 t almond extract
1/3 c hot water
4 1/2 c sesame seeds
2/3 c sliced almonds
2 1/2 c shredded coconut
1 t salt
3/4 c unbleached flour

Combine the honey, peanut butter (the kind with no additives), vanilla, almond extract, and water and beat until smooth and creamy. Add the dry ingredients, one at a time and stir.

Press the mixture into a papered 9" x 13" pan. Use cold water on your hands to help it not stick.

Bake for 25 minutes or until slightly browned. Cut into bars when almost cooled.

Brownies

Preheat oven to 375°
Makes a 9" x 13" pan

1 c butter
7 eggs
3 c sugar
1 c cocoa
2 t vanilla extract
3/4 c walnuts
2 1/4 c unbleached flour

Cream together the butter, sugar and eggs. Beat well until the mixture turns light. Add the vanilla, walnuts and cocoa. Stir. The air whipped in during the first step will help the brownies rise, so do not overbeat. Add the flour and stir.

Pour into a papered and oiled pan. Put in the oven and turn the oven down to 325°. Baking time is about 35 minutes. The brownies are done when they bounce back after a soft touch to the center. Wait until cool to cut.

Brownies Later

from Rosita's

Preheat oven to 375°
Makes a 9" x 13" pan

7 oz unsweetened chocolate
3/8 lb butter
6 eggs
3 c sugar
1 T vanilla extract
1 1/2 c flour
1/2 t salt
1 cup walnuts

Melt the chocolate and the butter in a stainless steel bowl over a pan of boiling water. Beat the eggs and the sugar together. Add the vanilla and stir. Add the chocolate mix and stir. Add the flour, salt and walnuts and stir. Pour the batter into a 9" x 13" baking pan which has been lined with paper and sprayed.

Place the pan in the oven and reduce heat to 350°. Baking time is about 35 minutes, until a toothpick comes out clean from the center.

Butterscotch Squares

Ronnie Bator's Mother

Preheat oven to 375°
Makes 2 dozen

1 1/4 c butter
5 eggs
5 c brown sugar
1/2 t salt
2 t vanilla extract
1 3/4 c roasted cashews
1 1/2 t baking powder
5 c flour

Whip together until light the oil, eggs and brown sugar. Add to this the salt, vanilla and roasted cashews. Stir until blended. It is not essential to roast the cashews first, but it does enhance their flavor. Add the flour cup by cup, stirring after each addition. Add the baking powder with the third or fourth cup of flour. Spread the mixture, which will be fairly dense, in a 10" x 15" baking pan which has been papered and sprayed or oiled.

Lower the oven temperature to 325° immediately after placing the pan in the oven. Baking time is about 30 minutes. Be careful to not overbake.

These are good with added chocolate or butterscotch chips.

Chewy Peanut Fingers

Alicia Donaldson

Makes about 2 dozen

1 c crunchy peanut butter
1/4 c honey
2 t vanilla extract
1/2 t salt
1 1/2 c powdered milk
1/2 c powdered sugar
1 c finely chopped pecans

In a bowl mix the peanut butter, honey and the vanilla. Add the salt, powdered milk and powdered sugar. Stir well. Shape into finger shapes and roll in the pecan pieces. Store these quick energy snacks in the refrigerator.

Cream Cheese Brownies

Shelly Shapiro

Preheat oven to 350°
Makes one dozen

- 4 oz semi sweet chocolate
- 5 T butter
- 3 oz cream cheese
- 1 c granulated sugar
- 3 eggs
- 1/2 c plus 1 T unbleached flour
- 1 1/2 t vanilla extract
- 1/2 t baking powder
- 1/2 t salt
- 1/4 t almond extract
- 1/2 c chopped walnuts

Melt the chocolate and 3 T butter in a small saucepan over very low heat. Stir while melting so the chocolate does not scorch. Set aside.

To make the cream cheese layer: Cream together the cream cheese and 2 T butter. Add 1/4 c sugar and whip until fluffy. Blend in the egg and 1/2 t vanilla. Stir in 1 T flour and set aside.

To finish the chocolate layer: Beat together 2 eggs and 3/4 c sugar. Stir in the chocolate mix, vanilla, almond extract and walnuts. Add the salt, baking powder and 1/2 c flour.

Spread half of the chocolate mixture in a 9" x 9" pan, which has been papered and oiled. Spread the cream cheese mixture over this. Add the second half of the chocolate mix on top. With a knife, marbleize the batter, then bake for about 35 minutes. When the brownies bounce back after a slight tap in the center, they are done.

Date Bars

Mom aka Peg Donaldson

Preheat oven to 350°
Makes 2 dozen

3 eggs
3/4 c sugar
1 1/2 c chopped dates
1 c chopped walnuts
1 t vanilla extract
1/4 t salt
1 t baking powder
1 1/4 c unbleached flour

powdered sugar

Thoroughly mix the eggs and the sugar. Add to this the dates, walnuts, vanilla and the salt. Next add the flour and the baking powder at the same time. Mix well until even textured. Pour the batter into a 9" x 13" pan which has been papered and oiled.

Bake for 30 minutes.

While still warm, cut into bars and roll in powdered sugar.

Healthy Fingers

Preheat oven to 325°
Makes 2 dozen

- 1/2 c honey
- 1/2 c peanut butter
- 1 T oriental sesame oil
- 1 t vanilla extract
- 1/2 c chopped pecans
- 1 T unbleached flour
- 2 T bran
- 1/4 c raisins
- 1 c rolled oats
- 2 c toasted sesame seeds

Toast the sesame seeds on a dry pan in the oven until they are golden. Stir occasionally. This enhances the flavor and allows them to be more easily digested.

Beat together the honey, peanut butter (the kind with no additives), sesame oil and and the vanilla. Add to this all of the dry ingredients, except the sesame seeds. Stir well.

Chill the mixture for at least an hour. Shape into slender fingers and roll in the sesame seeds. Store in the refrigerator.

Lebkuchen

Preheat oven to 350°
Makes 2 dozen

1 c honey
1 c molasses
1 1/2 c brown sugar
2 eggs
1 T lemon zest
2 T lemon juice
2 t cinnamon
1 t ground cloves
2 t nutmeg
1 c chopped walnuts
1 t baking soda
5 1/2 c unbleached flour

glaze

In a mixing bowl combine the honey, molasses, brown sugar, and the eggs. Whip until light. Add the lemon zest, lemon juice, the spices and the walnuts. Stir. Add the flour cup by cup, stirring after each addition. Add the baking soda with the second or third cup of flour. Mix thoroughly.

This fairly substantial dough should be patted into a 9" x 13" baking pan which has been lined with paper and oiled. Bake for about 35 minutes. Brush on Lebkuchen Glaze while still hot. Cut into bars.

QUICK SWEET BREADS

Apple Nut Bread

Ronnie Bator's Mother's Son

Preheat oven to 325°
Makes 2 medium loaves

1 c vegetable oil
2 c sugar
3 eggs
1 T cinnamon
2 t vanilla extract
3 medium apples,
finely chopped
2 c walnuts
1 1/2 baking soda
1/2 t salt
3 c unbleached flour

glaze

Thoroughly cream the butter, sugar and eggs. Add to this the vanilla, cinnamon, apples and the walnuts. Stir well. In a separate bowl, sift together the flour, baking soda and the salt. Stir these into the batter a cup at a time. The batter will be very stiff and still end up as a very moist bread because of the apples.

Divide this evenly between the loaf pans which have been oiled and lined with paper. Bake for about 1 1/4 hours. Test in the center with a toothpick.

After removing from the oven, allow to rest for a few minutes before removing the loaves from the pans. Glaze while still hot so there are drip marks running down all sides. Cool on a wire rack.

Apricot Bread

Preheat oven to 300°
Makes one loaf

1 1/2 c dried apricots
1 c water
3 eggs
1/3 c vegetable oil
3/4 c sugar
1 t vanilla extract
2 c unbleached flour
1 1/2 T baking powder
1/2 t salt
2/3 c pecan pieces

Place the apricots and the water in a small saucepan, cover and simmer over a low heat until the apricots are soft.

Thoroughly cream the eggs, oil and sugar. Add the vanilla and the apricot mix and blend until smooth. In a separate bowl mix the dry ingredients, including the pecans. Add the dry ingredients to the batter one cup at a time, stirring after each addition.

Pour the batter into a loaf pan which has been papered and oiled. Bake for about an hour. Cool on a wire rack.

Banananana Nut Bread

Jon Kronenberg's Aunt Marge Yochum

Preheat oven to 325° 360°
Makes one loaf
1 hr

- 1/2 c vegetable oil
- 1 c sugar
- 2 eggs
- 3 ripe banananas
- 1 t cinnamon
- 1/2 t ~~ground cloves~~ allspice
- 1 t baking soda 1/2
- 1/2 t baking powder - scant
- 2 c unbleached flour
- 1/2 c chopped ~~walnuts~~ pecans - Toast at 250° in sm. oven 6" turning/stirring every 2."

scant 1/2 tsp. salt
lemon juice to taste

Cream together the oil, sugar and eggs. Add the banananas and mash well. Add the cinnamon and cloves and stir.

Sift together the flour, baking soda, baking powder and the nuts. Stir the dry ingredients into the batter, cup by cup. After the batter is well blended, pour into a papered and oiled pan.

Bake for about an hour and a quarter and test with a toothpick.

Remove from the oven and place on a wire rack. If you choose to glaze the loaf, then do so while it is still hot.

BANANANA NUT BREAD

Boston Brown Bread

Grandma Jones

Preheat oven to 350°
Makes one loaf

1/4 c molasses
1/4 c sugar
1 T butter
1 egg
1 1/2 c buttermilk
1/2 t salt
1 c whole wheat flour
1 c unbleached flour
1 t baking soda
1 t baking powder
1/2 c raisins

Beat together the molasses, sugar, softened butter and the egg. They will grow smooth and light as you beat them.

Add all the dry ingredients in another bowl and stir them. Add these to the batter alternately with the buttermilk, stirring after each addition. Stir in the raisins.

Pour the batter into a loaf pan which has been papered and oiled. Place the loaf in the oven and reduce the temperature to 300. Bake for about an hour, then test the center of the loaf with a toothpick.

Allow to cool for a few minutes before removing the loaf from the pan. Cool on a wire rack.

Coconut Bread

For an event at the Contemporary Arts Center, New Orleans

Preheat oven to 325°
Makes one loaf

3 eggs
1/2 c vegetable oil
1 c sugar
1 1/3 c shredded coconut
1 t vanilla extract
1/2 t lemon extract
2 1/3 c unbleached flour
1 1/3 T baking powder
1/2 t salt
1 t cinnamon
1/2 t nutmeg
1 1/4 c milk

Thoroughly cream the eggs, oil and sugar. Add the coconut and the extracts and stir. Mix all of the dry ingredients in a separate bowl. Add the dry ingredients to the batter alternately with the milk. Stir after each addition.

Pour into a papered, oiled loaf pan and bake for about an hour.

After letting the loaf rest for a few minutes, remove from the pan and cool on a wire rack.

Cranberry Bread

Preheat oven to 325°
Makes one loaf

1/4 c vegetable oil
1 c sugar
1 egg
3/4 c orange juice
1 T orange zest
2 c chopped cranberries
1 1/2 t baking soda
1/2 t baking powder
1/2 t salt
2 c unbleached flour
1 c chopped walnuts

Begin by chopping and measuring the cranberries. Set aside. Next grate the orange zest and squeeze and measure the orange juice. Add the zest to the juice and set aside.

Thoroughly cream the vegetable oil, the sugar and the egg. When the mixture is light, add the cranberries and stir.

Sift together the flour, baking soda and powder and the salt. Stir the walnuts into the dry ingredients. Add the dry mix to the batter alternately with the orange juice. Stir well after each addition. The batter will be quite stiff.

Place the batter in a loaf pan which has been papered and oiled. Bake until a toothpick comes out clean from the center. Baking time is about 1 1/4 hours. Wait a few minutes before removing from the pan. If you choose to glaze the loaf, do it while still warm. Cool on a wire rack.

Date Nut Bread

Dean Betts' Aunt Alberta

Preheat oven to 350°
Makes 2 loaves

Prepare the oranges by rolling them on a counter under the pressure of your hand. Grate the zest, then juice the oranges. Pour the juice and the zest into a 2 cup measure. Add enough water to make 2 cups.

1/4 c vegetable oil
1 1/4 c sugar
2 eggs
2 t vanilla extract
2 c chopped dates
2 oranges
water
2 t baking soda
2 t baking powder
3/4 t salt
4 3/4 c unbleached flour
2 c chopped walnuts

In a mixing bowl, thoroughly cream the oil, sugar and eggs. When the mixture is light, measure in the vanilla and the dates and stir.

Sift together the flour, baking soda, baking powder and salt. Stir in the chopped walnuts. Alternately add the dry mix and the orange juice to the batter, stirring after each addition.

Pour the batter into two papered and oiled pans. After placing in the oven, reduce the temperature to 300°. Bake for about an hour and a half. Test the loaves with a toothpick. Wait a few minutes before removing from pans. If you wish to glaze the loaves, do it while they are still hot. The combination of flavors is tops.

Irish Soda Bread

Jackie McNulty Haber

Preheat oven to 375°
Makes one large loaf

4 c unbleached flour
1/4 c sugar
1 t salt
1 t baking powder
2 T caraway seeds
1/4 c butter
2 c raisins
1 egg
1 1/3 c buttermilk

1 egg yolk

Sift together the flour, sugar, salt, baking powder, and baking soda. Stir in the caraway seeds. Cut the softened butter into the mixture until it looks like coarse grained sand. Stir in the raisins. Beat the egg into the buttermilk, then stir into the dry ingredients, barely combining them.

Turn the dough onto a lightly floured counter and knead lightly about 5 minutes, until the dough is smooth. Shape into a ball and place in a well oiled round baking dish. With a serrated blade, slash an X on the top of the loaf. Brush the loaf with the egg yolk which has been beaten with a tablespoon of water.

Bake for about an hour or until a toothpick comes out clean from the center. Allow the loaf to set for several minutes before removing from the pan. Cool on a wire rack and cut in quarters before slicing to serve.

Lemon Pecan Bread

Preheat oven to 325°
Makes 1 loaf

1/3 c butter
1 c sugar
2 eggs
1/4 t almond extract
1 T lemon zest
3 T lemon juice
1/2 c milk
1 t baking powder
1/2 t salt
1 1/2 c unbleached flour
1/2 c chopped pecans

Thoroughly cream the butter, sugar and eggs. Add to this the almond extract, lemon juice and zest.

Sift together the flour, baking powder and salt. Stir the pecans into this dry mix. Add the dry mix to the batter alternately with the milk until all is evenly blended. The batter will be quite fluid and volatile. It is important to minimize the time between adding the milk and getting the loaf into the oven.

Pour the batter into an oiled and papered pan. Bake about an hour or until a toothpick comes out clean from the center of the loaf. Remove from the pan after allowing to rest for a few minutes. Glaze while still hot.

This bread is so good it is hard to believe anyone would make just one loaf.

Pumpkin Bread

Preheat oven to 325°
Makes 1 loaf

1/3 c vegetable oil
1 c sugar
1 c pumpkin
1 1/3 c water
1/2 t vanilla extract
1/2 t cinnamon
1/2 t nutmeg
2 c unbleached flour
1 t baking soda
1/4 t baking powder
3/4 t salt
1/2 c raisins
1/2 c chopped pecans

Cream the butter, sugar, and eggs thoroughly. Stir in the pumpkin, water, vanilla, cinnamon and nutmeg. Beat until smooth.

Let's talk about the pumpkin: fresh is the best by far. I dare you to try it. The color is lighter and the taste of fresh pumpkin lacks that metal edge of canned. It isn't that hard to cut up a pumpkin. Feed the seeds to yourself and friends, or the birds. Steam it in a kettle. Let it cool. Puree it in a food processor. Put it in ziplock bags in the freezer for the whole year. It's good for pies, soups, bread, muffins. Really, I dare you.

Mix the flour, baking powder, baking soda, salt, raisins and nuts together in a separate bowl. Gradually incorporate this dry mixture into the batter.

Pour the batter into an oiled and papered pan. Bake for about an hour. Allow a few minutes to cool before removing from the pan. Cool on a wire rack.

Zucchini Bread

Mrs. Worrall Hess, Sr.

Preheat oven to 325°
Makes 2 loaves

- 1 3/4 c sugar
- 4 eggs
- 1 c vegetable oil
- 1 t vanilla extract
- 2 c grated zucchini
- 3 1/2 c unbleached flour
- 1 t baking powder
- 1 1/2 t baking soda
- 1 1/2 t salt
- 1 T cinnamon
- 1 c raisins
- 1 c chopped walnuts

Beat the eggs. Add the sugar and oil, then cream until smooth and light. With a few strokes, mix the vanilla and the grated zucchini into the batter.

In a separate bowl, measure the flour, baking soda, baking powder, salt, and cinnamon. Stir these together. Add the walnuts and the raisins to this dry mix.
Stir once again.

Gradually add the dry ingredients to the batter, mixing until an even texture is obtained. Pour the batter into 2 loaf pans which have been oiled and lined with paper.

Bake about an hour or until the loaves bounce back in the center to a light touch. Allow to set for a few minutes before removing from the pans. Cool on a wire rack.

BREADS & ROLLS

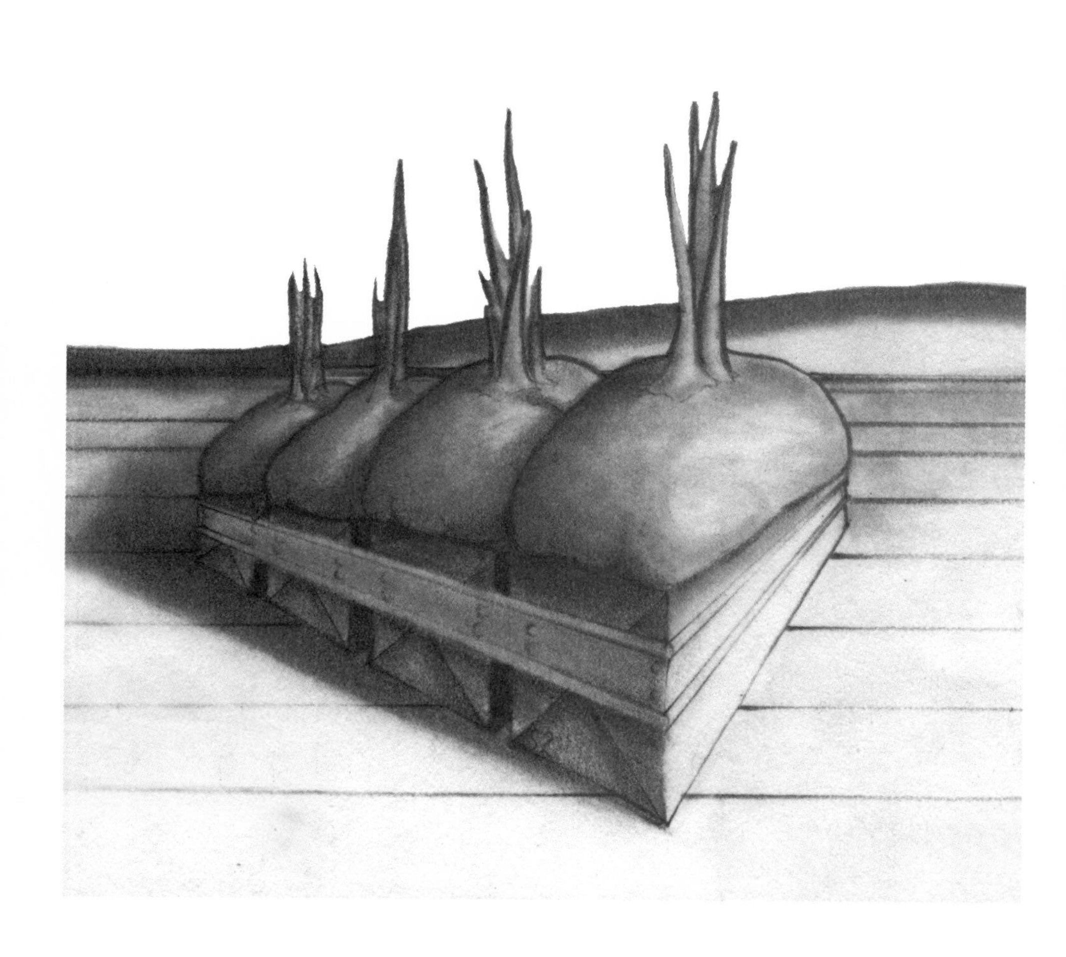

The Wheats

(Unannounced guests with dinner ringing and the phone burning)

Undoubtedly upon your mind
the tragic wheats, their presence find.
Don't think concern is yours alone,
I sleep frustrated now at home.
At first I held my hopes so high —
The bubbling softly whispered sigh
Gave every reasonable indication
Tonight the breads would rise to occasion.
Things looked so good for a while,
To the breads I betrayed a satisfied smile;
And sitting back in a moment's applause,
The loaves abandoned the bakery's cause.
Maliciously, they had the gall,
When placed in the oven to mockingly fall.
Heartfelt dismay was mine half an hour later.
My wheats held all the beauty of an old alligator.

Much as I wish to clutch at fate.
I fear I put them in too late;
so much preliminary size
undoubtedly was all they'd rise.
What can I say for all my yearning,
Bru, but the wheats I am still learning.

S. Doug Hettinger

Beer Bread

Denny Ash

Bake at 350°
Makes 2 loaves

1 1/2 c warm beer
1/3 c bacon grease
1/3 c molasses
1 T caraway seeds
2 T yeast
1/3 c water
6 c whole wheat flour
2 t salt

Combine in a large mixing bowl the warm beer, bacon grease, molasses and caraway seed. Make sure they are warm enough to promote the growth of the yeast colony.

Dissolve the yeast in the water, again quite warm is a good idea, but not hot. Stir well, then let it rest until the yeast rises to the surface and gets foamy. Add this to the mixing bowl. Add three cups of flour and beat one hundred strokes. Cover and set aside for about 15 minutes.

Beat the mixture down to about its original size. Add the salt and one cup of flour. Stir. Gradually add the rest of the flour. When the dough becomes too stiff to stir, then turn onto a lightly floured counter and knead for a few minutes. Return the dough to the mixing bowl. Cover and set aside to double.

Punch down the dough. Knead until smooth and shape into loaves. Place the loaves in oiled, lightly floured pans. When the loaves have doubled in size, place them in a preheated 350° oven for about 40 minutes. Allow to rest for a few minutes before removing from the pans. Cool on a wire rack.

Cardamom Rolls

Inspiration at Dean's Sea of Cortez

Bake at 350°
Makes 2 dozen rolls

- 2 c water
- 2/3 c vegetable oil
- 1/2 c honey
- 2 eggs
- 3 T yeast
- 1 T cardamom
- 1 T cinnamon
- 1 t salt
- 5 c unbleached flour
- 4 c rye flour

In a large mixing bowl, combine the water, honey and oil. Sprinkle in the yeast while stirring. Stir until dissolved. Let this rest while the yeast grows. When the yeast rises to the surface, add half of each kind of flour and beat for at least one hundred strokes. Let it rest for ten minutes.

Stir down the dough sponge. Add the eggs, which have been beaten with a fork in a cup. Add the cinnamon, cardamom and salt. Add one cup of flour to this and then stir well. Add the flour, cup by cup, until it is too stiff to stir. Turn onto a lightly floured counter and knead. Return the dough to the bowl, cover, and allow to rise to doubled, or about 30 minutes.

Punch down the dough. Gently knead to remove any air pockets.

Divide the dough and shape into little round rolls. Place the rolls on a papered tray and set aside to double. Preheat the oven to 350° and bake for about 20 minutes or until nicely browned.

The flavor of these rolls blends extremely well with a variety of seafoods.

Cheese Bread

Bruce Littlefield and his beloved Mom

Preheat oven to 375°
Bake at 350°

- 2 T butter
- 4 T unbleached flour
- 1 c milk
- 1 1/4 c grated sharp cheddar
- 1 T honey
- 1/4 c water
- 1 T yeast
- 3 c unbleached flour
- 1 t salt

Melt the butter in a sauce pan or double boiler or stainless steel bowl over a pan of boiling water. Gradually add the 4 T of flour, alternately with a bit of the milk, stirring often to avoid lumps. Continue stirring and add the rest of the milk. Cook this mixture until thick. Add the cheese and stir occasionally until the cheese is melted and a thick sauce is achieved. Set aside the sauce to cool until it is warm but not hot.

Add the honey to the 1/4 cup of warm water. Sprinkle in the yeast and stir until it is dissolved. Allow it to sit until it starts to foam. Pour this into a mixing bowl and stir in a bit of the flour. Beat well. Add the cheese sauce and a cup of flour. Stir until smooth. Add the rest of the flour a cup at a time and the salt. When the dough becomes too stiff to knead, turn onto a lightly floured counter and knead until smooth. Return the dough to the bowl, cover, and allow to rise until doubled.

Punch down the dough, knead until smooth, and shape into a loaf. Place the loaf in a lightly oiled pan and allow to double. Preheat the oven to 375°. Place the loaf in the oven. After 5 minutes, reduce the heat to 350°. Baking time is about 40 minutes. Remove from the pan and allow to cool, if you can stand to wait any longer before eating. This bread is terrific, plain, toasted or for great sandwiches.

Dark Rye

Bake at 350°
Makes 2 loaves

2 1/2 c water
3 T oil
2 T honey
1/4 c molasses
2 1/2 T yeast
3 T caraway seeds
1/4 c cocoa
5 c unbleached flour
1 T salt
4 c rye flour

When using rye flour it is important to remember that rye does not contain gluten. Gluten is the elastic bonding material which holds in the bubbles and allows bread to have the structure it has. That's why a combination of flours is used. Do not overbeat, over-rise, or knead for too long.

In a large mixing bowl, combine the water, honey and molasses. Stir in the yeast. After the yeast has dissolved, let the mix sit until the yeast rises to the surface and begins to foam. While you are waiting, measure half of each kind of flour. After the yeast has risen, add the oil and then the measured flour and beat for about a hundred strokes. Allow this to rise for about ten minutes.

Add the cocoa, caraway seeds, salt and a cup of each kind of flour and stir well. Keep adding flour until the dough is too stiff to stir. Turn the dough onto a lightly floured counter and gradually work in the rest of the flour. If the dough is sticky and needs more flour, use unbleached. Knead long enough to create a smooth dough. Set the dough aside to rise for about 30 minutes.

Punch down the dough. Knead lightly, then divide into halves, Shape into round loaves, score the tops with X marks. Set the loaves on papered cornmeal covered trays. Allow to rise until almost doubled. Preheat the oven to 350° and bake for about 40 minutes. Whap the loaves and listen for a hollow sound to see if they are done.

Egg Bagels, Plain or Onion

Bake at 375°
Makes about 2 dozen

2 1/2 c water
1/4 c honey
2 T yeast
1 egg
2 t salt
12 c unbleached flour

1 T salt
1 diced onion
poppy seeds
sesame seeds

Pour the 2 1/2 c water into a very large mixing bowl. Dissolve the honey in the water and then stir in the yeast, continuing to stir until dissolved. Let this mix sit undisturbed while 6 cups of flour are measured. As soon as the yeast rises to the surface, pour in the flour and beat until smooth and shiny.

Allow to rise for 10 minutes. Add the beaten egg and the salt with a cup of flour and beat well. Gradually work in the rest of the flour. When it becomes too difficult to stir, turn onto a lightly floured counter and knead. The dough will be fairly stiff. Cover and allow to sit for just a few minutes.

Choose a pan with a large diameter. Fill with water to about 1 1/2 to 2 inches from the rim. Add about 1 T salt and bring the water to a boil.

To shape the bagels, divide into pieces and shape into 3" balls. After you have done that, start with the one shaped first and poke a hole in it. Twirl it around your fingers. Place it on the counter and flatten with the palm of your hand.

Preheat the oven. Place the bagels, a few at a time, in the boiling water. After they rise to the surface, they need to stay in the water only about 20 to 30 seconds. Remove from the water with tongs or a slotted spoon. Place on a papered tray. Immediately add seeds, if desired. Bake about 20 minutes or until golden.

If onions are desired, add a finely diced onion to the dough at the same time you add the egg and salt. Onion dough will require more flour.

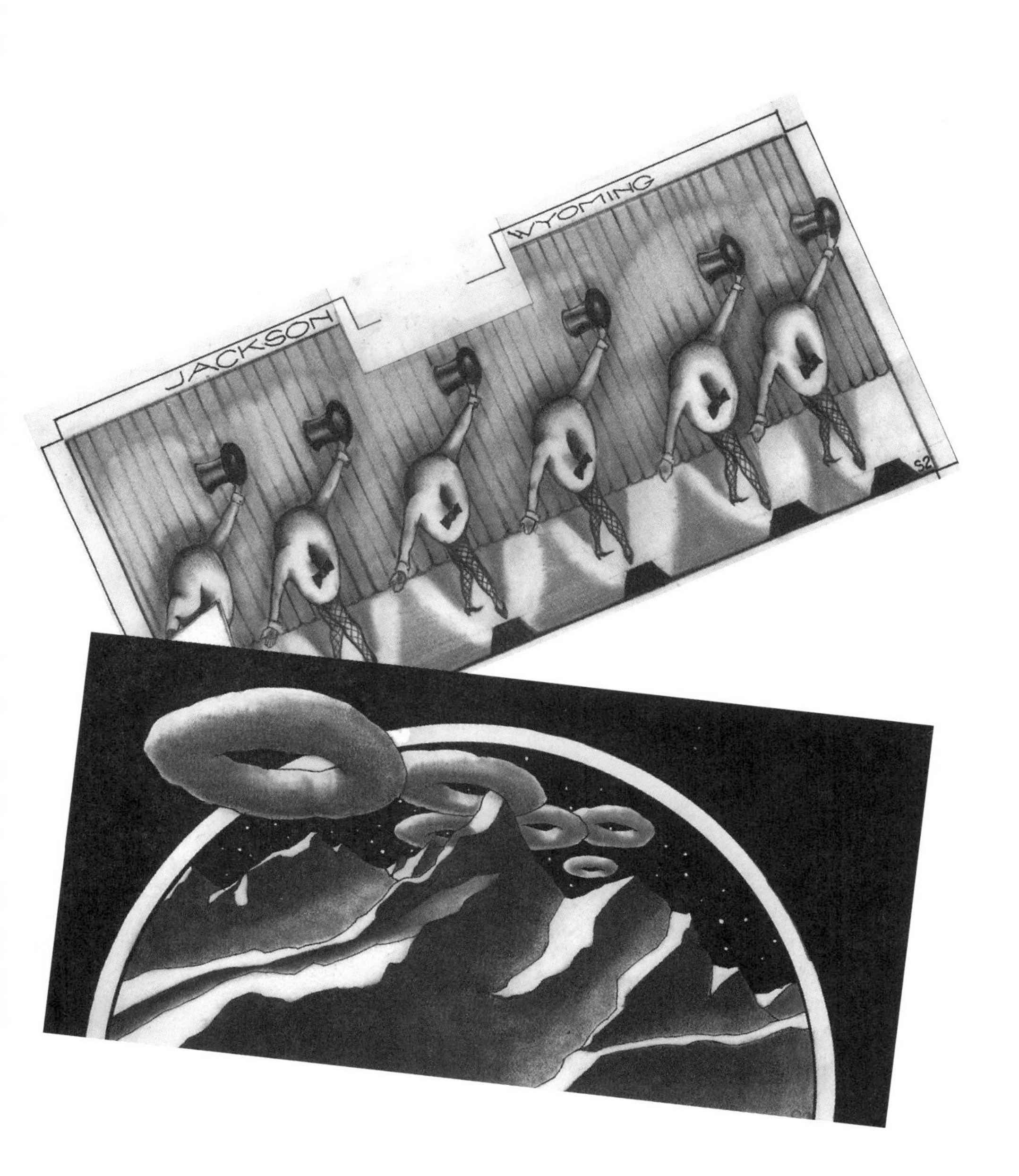
JACKSON
WYOMING

English Muffins

Cook on a dry griddle or cast iron skillet
Makes 1 dozen

1 1/2 c scalded milk
1 T honey
1 T yeast
1 t salt
1 c whole wheat flour
2 1/4 c unbleached flour

cornmeal

Scald the milk, then pour it into a large mixing bowl. Stir in the honey. When this is cooled to about 100° or the perfect temperature for bath water, sprinkle in the yeast and stir until dissolved. Add the wheat flour and one cup of the unbleached after the yeast has risen to the surface and begun to look foamy. Beat for about 100 strokes, set aside, covered, and let rest for 10 minutes.

Add the salt and gradually work in the remainder of the flour. Knead lightly for about 5 minutes. Cover and let rest for about 20 minutes.

Punch down the dough and knead lightly and briefly. Place on a counter dusted with cornmeal. Roll the dough to about 3/4 inch thick. Cut with a round cutter about 4" in diameter. Cover these and let them rise for about 15 minutes.

Preheat the skillet or griddle to a medium low heat. Carefully transfer the muffins to the dry cooking surface. The muffins will take about 15 minutes to cook. Handle them very gently, but rotate them and turn them over for even browning. Transfer them to a towel lined basket and serve or cool and store.

I recall a summer solstice champagne brunch birthday party for a couple dozen people at our campfire. We had Eggs Benedict on these muffins. They have never tasted better.

Light Rye

From a Wild Winds inspiration

Bake at 350°
Makes 2 loaves

- 2 c water
- 1/4 c oil
- 1/3 c honey
- 2 1/2 T yeast
- 2 T dill weed
- 2 T dill seed
- 4 c unbleached flour
- 2 t salt
- 4 c rye flour

In a large mixing bowl, combine the warm water and the honey. Sprinkle in the yeast and stir until dissolved. Before the yeast rises to the surface, measure the oil. In another bowl measure and stir together both kinds of flour and the seasonings.

As the yeast rises to the surface, add the oil and pour in about 4 cups of the flour mix. Stir about 100 strokes and set aside for 10 to 15 minutes.

Beat down the batter and add more flour, cup by cup until it is easier to knead than stir. Turn onto a lightly floured counter and knead about 5 minutes. Cover and let rise until doubled in a warm place.

Punch down the dough and knead lightly. Shape into loaves. Place the loaves in lightly oiled pans and let them rise until doubled. Preheat the oven and then bake about 40 minutes. The loaves will be golden brown and sound hollow when lightly tapped. Remove from the pans for cooling.

Logan Bread

Preheat oven to 275°
Makes 2 loaves

6 eggs
2 T oil
1/2 c honey
1/4 c molasses
1/2 c maple syrup
2 c rye flour
2 1/2 c wheat flour
1/2 c powdered milk
1/2 c chopped pecans
2/3 c raisins
1/2 c coconut

Logan Bread is an extremely substantial little item. It is the perfect bread to take on long and arduous expeditions. It is compact and durable and very nutritious. It keeps for long periods of time. I learned to make it because my buddies talked me into it. I still have photos from somewhere on Mt. Hunter with my buddies standing by a tent staked down with little loaves of breads from my ovens.

In a large bowl mix together all of the dry ingredients.

In a different bowl, beat the eggs until they are light. Add the liquids, continuing to beat until you form a well blended mixture.

Gradually work in all of the dry ingredients to form a dense, sticky dough. Transfer the dough to papered, well oiled loaf pans. Bake for about 2 hours. After the first hour reduce the heat to 225°. Test with a toothpick to the center of the loaves. Cool on a wire rack before wrapping well for freezing or travel.

Oatmeal Sunflower Millet Bread

Bake at 350°
Makes 2 loaves

2 1/4 c water
2 1/2 T yeast
1/2 c honey
5/8 c safflower oil
1 1/2 T salt
1/2 c rolled oats
1/4 c sunflower seeds
1/4 c millet
6 1/2 c whole wheat flour

Into a large mixing bowl measure the water, which needs to be quite warm. Stir in the honey. Sprinkle in the yeast and stir until dissolved. While the yeast is growing, measure the oil. When the yeast rises to the surface and starts to foam, add 3 cups of the flour and beat for a hundred strokes. The batter will look smooth and glossy. Cover and let rest for twenty minutes.

Add the oatmeal, sunflower seeds, millet and salt. Stir down the spongy dough. Add one cup of the remaining flour and stir well. Gradually add the rest of the flour. When the dough becomes too stiff to stir, turn onto a lightly floured counter and knead for about 10 minutes. The amount of flour will vary from day to day, depending on weather. The dough will be soft, but not sticky. Cover the dough and allow to rise until doubled.

Punch down the dough and knead lightly for about 5 minutes. Shape into loaves. Place in papered and lightly oiled pans and allow to rise until doubled. Preheat the oven and bake for about 40 minutes.The loaves will be nicely browned and sound hollow when tapped. Cool on a wire rack.

Onion Rolls

Bake at 375°
Makes 1 1/2 dozen

- 2 c water
- 3 T honey
- 1 1/2 T yeast
- 1/2 c oil
- 8 c unbleached flour
- 2/3 c finely diced onion
- 1 T salt

egg wash

In a large mixing bowl combine the water and the honey. Sprinkle in the yeast and stir until dissolved. Let rest for a few minutes while you measure the oil. After the yeast rises to the surface, add the oil and half of the flour. Beat for at least 50 strokes and set aside to rise for 10 minutes.

Add the onion and the salt and a cup of flour. Stir. Gradually add the remaining flour, stirring in after each addition. Turn the dough onto a lightly floured counter and knead gently. The dough will be moist and sticky if kneaded too intensely. Keep adding flour. Set aside to rise until doubled.

Prepare an egg wash in a cup by beating a tablespoon of water into the egg. Punch down the dough. Knead gently on a floured counter to rid the dough of air pockets, adding flour if necessary. Shape the dough into smooth ovals about 5" x 2 1/2" and about 3/4" thick. Place the rolls on a papered tray and brush with the egg wash. Preheat the oven while the rolls double in size. Bake for about 25 minutes or until the rolls are nicely browned. Let them cool before using to make great sandwiches.

SZ

Pizza Dough

Bake at 400°
Makes 4 rounds

1 1/2 c water
4 T olive oil
1 T honey or sugar
1 1/2 T yeast
1 finely minced garlic clove
1 t salt
4 c unbleached flour

Because I am asked sooooo often, I am including this recipe.

In a mixing bowl, combine the very warm water and the sweetener. Sprinkle in the yeast and stir until dissolved. When it rises to the surface, add the oil and salt and one cup of flour. Beat well. Add the garlic which is very finely minced or put through a press. Gradually add the rest of the flour and knead lightly for a few minutes. Let the dough rest for 10 to 15 minutes while you assemble the topping ingredients.

Shape into four rounds. Pat the dough or lightly roll the dough into pizzas about 1/2 to 3/4 inch thick. Make sure they are not sticky on the bottom, keeping them dusted with flour before placing on a flat sheet. Top with anything you want. Leave a ring with no toppings about 1/2 inch around the perimeter. Place in the preheated oven.

They will take about 20 minutes to bake. Move them from bottom to top shelf. After baking about half of the time, carefully remove the tray so the pizzas sit on the oven rack. This is the way to get them browned on the bottom. Slip the tray back under the pizza to remove from the oven. Place on a cutting board to slice.

Ragbrod

from Ernie

Bake at 375°
Makes 2 loaves

1 c water
2 T butter
1/2 c molasses
6 T orange zest
2 T fennel seeds
2 T caraway seeds
1/4 c water
2 1/2 T yeast
2 c buttermilk
4 c rye flour
5 c unbleached flour
1 t baking soda
1 T salt

In a sauce pan combine 1 c water, the butter, molasses, orange zest, fennel, and caraway seeds and bring to a boil. Allow this mix to cool to bath temperature before continuing.

In a large mixing bowl, dissolve the yeast in 1/4 c warm water. Allow the yeast to sit undisturbed for several minutes. Add the sauce, the buttermilk and half of each kind of flour. Beat for at least 50 strokes. Allow this to sit undisturbed for 10 minutes. Add the baking soda, salt and one cup of the unbleached flour and stir until smooth. Gradually work in the rest of the flour. When the dough is too stiff to stir, turn onto a lightly floured counter and knead for about 5 minutes. Return to the bowl and cover or lightly oil the crust before allowing the dough to rise for 30 minutes.

Punch down the dough. Knead gently for long enough to remove the air holes. Shape into 2 round loaves. Place on papered trays. Slash the tops of the loaves with X's. Allow to rise until doubled. Preheat the oven. Bake for about 40 minutes. To create a firmer crust you may brush the loaves with water or spray them with water after about 20 minutes of baking.

Sourdough French

Bake at 450°
Makes 3 loaves

1 c water
1 T honey
1 T yeast
1 c starter
1 T salt
4 c unbleached flour
3 1/2 c high gluten flour

In a large mixing bowl dissolve the honey in the warm water. Sprinkle in the yeast and stir until dissolved. As the yeast begins to foam add the starter. Add half of each kind of flour and beat well. When the mix is smooth and shiny, cover and set aside to rise until doubled.

Add the salt and one cup of each kind of flour and beat well. Gradually add the rest of the flour. When it is too stiff to stir, turn onto a lightly floured counter and knead well. Return to the bowl, cover and let rise until doubled.

Punch down and knead well. Shape into slender loaves and place on papered trays. Slash the top of the loaves with a series of diagonal lines. You may want to brush the loaves with an egg wash. Let the loaves double in size.

Preheat the oven. Place the loaves in the oven. Throw a couple of ice cubes on the oven floor and shut the door. Or instead of the ice cubes, after about 5 minutes of baking spray the loaves with water from a squirt bottle. These steaming procedures help form a good crust. The loaves will be done in about 20 minutes. They will be golden brown and sound hollow when tapped.

Sourdough Rye

Bake at 475°
Makes 2 loaves

1 1/2 c water
1 1/2 T yeast
1 c starter
5-6 c rye flour
3 c unbleached flour
4 c high gluten flour
1 1/2 T salt
2 T caraway seeds

Pour the warm water into a large mixing bowl. Sprinkle in the yeast and stir until dissolved. After the yeast has risen to the surface, add the sourdough starter. Add half of each kind of flour. Beat at least one hundred strokes. Cover and set aside in a warm place to double.

After the dough has doubled, add the caraway seeds and the salt and beat down. Gradually add the rest of the flours. Stir until it becomes too difficult and then turn onto a lightly floured counter and knead. Keep adding flour and kneading until the dough is extremely stiff. Cover and set aside to double. This could take hours, overnight even.

After the dough has risen, punch down and turn onto a lightly floured counter and knead well. Add more flour if necessary. Shape into oval loaves and place on a papered tray. Slash the tops of the loaves with a series of diagonal lines. Allow to rise until doubled.

Preheat the oven. Place the loaves in the oven. Throw a handful of ice cubes on the oven floor and close the door. Another way to create steam for a good crust is to spray the loaves with a squirt bottle of water after a few minutes of baking. After about 20 minutes of baking take the loaves from the oven and brush with an egg wash.

Baking time will be about 40 minutes. Close to the end of the bake, you may repeat either steaming procedure. The loaves will be nicely browned and hollow sounding when they are done.

Sourdough Starter

2 c water
2 T sugar
2 T yeast
2 c unbleached flour

Boil the water and then allow it to cool to bath temperature. Add the sugar and stir until dissolved. Sprinkle in the yeast and stir until dissolved. Add the flour and beat well. Cover loosely. Let it sit for at least a day at room temperature. This mixture is alive. You do not have to use any sweetener at all, it will just take longer for the yeast colony to develop.

A crock is a good container for keeping sourdough, as it holds temperature well. The size of the crock needs to be at least twice as large as the volume of starter.

Feed it every day. While you are getting a starter going, remove half of it (which is quite a good bacterial colony to put down a garbage disposal or a toilet). Add one cup of warm water and one cup of flour. Repeat this for several days. The consistency is like a thick milkshake.

Yeast is killed if it gets as hot as 140°. It will stay alive if it is frozen. It grows more slowly when it is cool. It is happiest when about 100°.

It's a great idea to keep some starter in the freezer as a back up. It keeps in a refrigerator for many weeks. Whenever you use starter, let it warm to room temperature and feed it and let it sit for at least an hour first.

If it changes color or odor, throw it out.

Sourdough has many uses in cakes, pancakes, waffles and breads.

Spinach Loaf

Barbara Sanford Smith

Bake at 425° for 10 minutes then 350°
Makes 1 loaf

1 1/2 c water
2 T olive oil
1 1/2 T honey
1 T yeast
1 beaten egg
1 finely minced clove of garlic
1 t salt
4 1/2 c unbleached flour

olive oil
grated romano
grated mozzarella
chopped spinach
diced onion
chopped olives

In a large bowl combine the warm water, olive oil and honey. Sprinkle in the yeast and stir until dissolved. When the yeast rises to the surface, add the beaten egg, the salt and the garlic. Add half of the flour and beat for one hundred strokes. Let rest for 10 minutes.

Gradually add the rest of the flour until a soft dough is formed. Turn onto a lightly floured counter and knead gently for a few minutes. Return to the bowl, cover and let rise for about 15 minutes.

Punch down. Turn onto a lightly floured counter and gently knead for just a few minutes. Dust with flour and roll into a rectangle about 1/2 inch thick. Brush with olive oil. The choices of fillings are all optional. Cover the dough with grated cheese. Sprinkle with chopped, fresh spinach, diced onions and olives. Roll the dough into a tight roll and pinch the edges together. Place on a papered tray with the seam on the bottom.

Preheat the oven to 425°. After the oven is hot, put the loaf in to bake. After 10 minutes, reduce the heat to 350° and bake for another half hour or until the loaf is nicely browned. Enjoy it hot or cold.

Tortillas

Rhonda Robles

Cook on a dry griddle
or cast iron pan
Makes 1 dozen

4 c flour
1 T salt
2/3 c bacon grease
shortening or oil
1 c warm water

In a large mixing bowl measure the flour and salt. Mix together with your hands. Add the bacon grease, or oil-like product of your choice, by rubbing between your hands and fingers. It should be quite well blended before adding the water. Make a well in the center of your mix. Pour the warm water into the well. Mix until a dough is formed. A bit more water might be needed to make a soft dough, depending of the weather.

Turn onto a slightly floured counter and knead for about ten minutes. Cover with a towel and let the dough rest for about 15 minutes. Knead for a few minutes before starting to roll. Twist off a piece of dough, about 1 /12. Shape it with your fingers to make it as flat and round as possible. Put this circle on a counter that you keep lightly floured. Using a rolling pin, roll once over the tortilla and once back. Turn the tortilla over and rotate it 1/3 of the way around. Roll back and forth and flip it and rotate it one third again. Repeat the rolling, rotating flipping process until the tortilla is quite thin.

Heat a griddle or a large cast iron skillet to medium heat. Turn the tortilla onto the dry pan. Cook on the first side until the color changes from translucent to more opaque. Turn over with a spatula or by hand. Cook on the second side and then flip over again. They may puff up while baking. They will have brown spots. If they get too dark, then the heat is too high. They look like craters on the moon to a vivid imagination.

Well wrapped tortillas keep for many days. They may be reheated in the same way they were cooked.

Whole Wheat

Bake at 350°
Makes 2 loaves

2 1/4 c water
1/2 c honey
2/3 c vegetable oil
2 1/2 T yeast
1 T salt
7 c whole wheat flour

In a large mixing bowl combine the warm water and the honey. Stir until the honey is dissolved. Sprinkle in the yeast and stir until dissolved. Allow to rest until the yeast rises to the surface and begins to foam. Measure in the oil and half of the flour. Beat at least one hundred strokes. Cover with a cloth and allow to rest for 15 to 20 minutes.

Add the salt and a cup of flour and stir down. Add the remaining flour gradually and stir until the dough becomes too stiff. Turn onto a lightly floured counter and knead for several minutes. The dough needs to be moist but not sticky. The amount of flour will vary with the weather.

After the dough is well kneaded, set aside, covered, to allow to rise until doubled. Punch down. Knead gently to remove the air holes and sweeten the smell of the dough. Shape into two loaves or various sized dinner or sandwich rolls. Place in loaf pans or on papered trays. Let rise until doubled.

Preheat the oven to 350°. Bake loaves for about 35 to 40 minutes. Rolls take less time. They will be well browned when done.

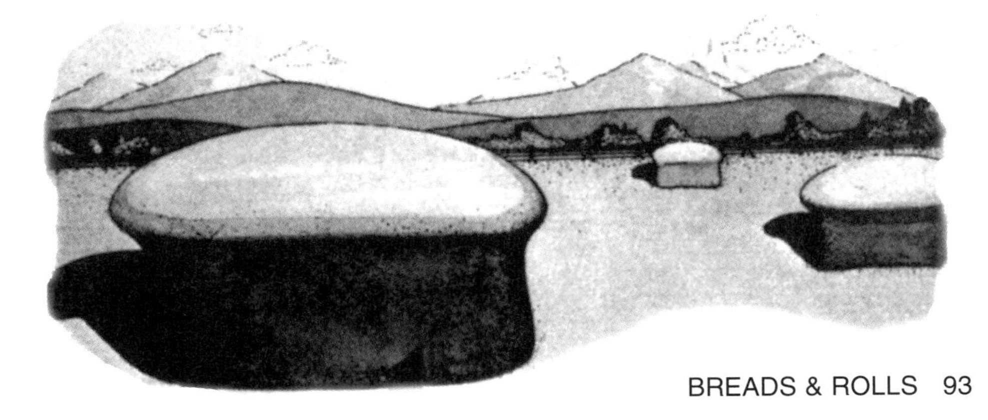

CANDY

Divinity

Jon Kronenberg, the Baron

Makes 40 1" squares

1/3 c light corn syrup
1/4 c water
1 1/8 c sugar
1 egg white
1/4 t salt
1/4 c chopped pecans
1/2 t vanilla extract

cup of cold water
butter
powdered sugar

Bring the water and the corn syrup to a boil in a covered saucepan. Remove from the heat and stir in the sugar. Return to the heat and bring to a boil, continue boiling without stirring on as low a heat as possible. Remove from the heat when a drop of this mixture does not change shape when dropped into a cup of cold water.

Beat the egg white until stiff. Stir the egg white and the salt into the syrup mixture. Place the pan in a sink of cold water and stir until the glossiness is gone.

Stir in the pecans and the vanilla. Pour the mixture onto a buttered stoneware platter or marble slab. After it has cooled, the divinity may be cut into squares, rolled in powdered sugar and wrapped.

English Toffee

Becky Stone

Makes 2 dozen 1" squares

2 c unsalted butter
1/2 c water
2 c sugar
1 T corn syrup
3/4 c chopped almonds
1 oz bitter chocolate
2 T sugar

butter
almond pieces

Bring to a boil in a covered saucepan the butter, water and corn syrup. After this has boiled, remove from the heat and stir in the 2 cups of sugar until it dissolves. Return to the heat and again cover and bring to a boil. Remove the cover and pour in the almonds. Reduce the heat to medium and continue boiling until the mixture smokes. It is important that it not be covered. It is also important not to stir.

Pour the smoking mixture onto a buttered stoneware platter or a slab of marble.

Melt the chocolate with the 2 tablespoons of sugar. Spread the chocolate over the toffee. Sprinkle with almond pieces which are finely chopped. Cut when cooled.

Penuche

Makes 40 1" squares

2/3 c cream
2 T butter
1 c brown sugar
1 1/2 c sugar
1 t vanilla extract
1/2 c finely chopped walnuts

butter

In a covered saucepan heat the butter and cream to boiling. Remove from the heat and stir in the sugars. Return to the heat and bring to a boil, again covered. When the sugar crystals on the sides of the pan dissolve, remove the cover, reduce the heat, and cook gently until a drop of the mixture holds its shape when dropped in a glass of cold water.

Cool without stirring until the pan feels luke warm. Add the walnuts and the vanilla. Beat with a wooden spoon until the mixture loses its gloss. Pour onto a buttered stoneware platter or a marble slab.
Cut when cool.

Sesame Crunch

Preheat oven to 300°
Makes 1 dozen squares

1 1/2 c sesame seeds
1 1/2 c honey
1 T cider vinegar
1/4 t salt

glass of cold water

Place the sesame seeds on a dry pan and toast until golden. Do not burn them. Boil the honey, vinegar and salt together until a drop of this syrup holds its shape when dropped into a glass of cold water. Pour the seeds into the mix and stir. Pour into an oiled baking dish and flatten. Cut into squares while still warm.

CAKES & MUFFINS

Banana Cake

Preheat oven to 350°
Makes 2 9" layers

3/4 c butter
1 c sugar
2 eggs
1 c bananas, mashed
1 t vanilla extract
1 7/8 c unbleached flour
1 t salt
1 t baking soda
1/2 t cinnamon
1/4 t ground cloves
1/3 c milk

Thoroughly cream the butter and sugar. Add the eggs, one at a time, beating until light. Add the cup of mashed bananas and the vanilla. Stir until smooth. Measure sifted flour into a separate bowl. Stir into the flour the salt, baking soda, cinnamon and cloves.

Add the dry mix and the milk to the batter. Stir until evenly mixed.

Pour the batter into the layer pans which have been lined with paper and lightly oiled. Bake for about 35 minutes or until the cake bounces back to a light touch in the center or a toothpick comes out clean from the center.

Basic Yellow Cake

Preheat oven to 350°
Makes 2 9" layers

3/4 c butter
1 1/2 c sugar
3 eggs
1 t vanilla extract
1 1/4 c milk
1/2 t salt
2 t baking powder
2 3/4 c unbleached flour

Thoroughly cream the butter and sugar. Add the eggs, one at a time, and beat well after each addition.

Sift the flour before measuring into a separate bowl. Stir the salt and the baking powder into the flour. Add the milk and the dry ingredients alternately. Beat well. Pour the batter into the layer pans which have been lined with paper and lightly oiled.

Bake about 35 minutes or until the layers spring back in the center in response to a light touch.

This basic cake may be frosted with any kind of frosting or covered with whipped cream and strawberries.

Black Forest Cake

Refrigerate after assembling

2 oz kirsch
4 oz grated bittersweet chocolate
3 c sweetened whipped cream
3 c pitted cherries
2 9" chocolate cake layers

This delicious cake is quite fragile and perishable. It helps if all of the ingredients are chilled.

Either the Hundred Dollar Cake or the Devil's Food Cake will work well for creating the chocolate layers. When the layers have been thoroughly cooled, cut them in half laterally to create four delicately thin layers. Fill a spray bottle with the kirsch and spray all of the layers.

Place one layer on a cake plate. Spread with the chilled whipped cream about 1/2 inch thick. Cover the layer with well drained cherries. Place on the next layer and repeat the process until all four layers are stacked. Cover the whole outside of the cake with whipped cream. Cover the sides of the cake with chocolate shavings. Reserve a few chocolate shavings for the center of the top. Place a ring of cherries around the outer edge of the top, one on each slice.

Refrigerate until serving.

Blueberry Bran Muffins

Shena Waugh Sandler

Preheat oven to 375°
Makes 2 dozen

1 1/4 c boiling water
3 c bran
2 eggs
1/2 c oil
1 c honey
2 c buttermilk
2 c unbleached flour
1/2 t salt
1/2 t baking soda
2 c blueberries

In a mixing bowl, pour the boiling water over the bran. Wait a few minutes. Add the eggs and beat well. Next add the honey and the oil, again beating well. Mix the baking soda and the salt into the flour. Add the buttermilk and the dry mix to the batter alternately, stirring well after all are added. Delicately mix the blueberries into the batter. Don't allow the batter to turn blue.

Fill paper lined muffin tins or well oiled muffin tins with the batter. Fill to about 2/3 full. Bake about 25 minutes or until the centers bounce back after a soft touch.

Cajun Style Corn Muffins

Preheat oven to 400°
Makes 1 dozen

- 1 1/2 c unbleached flour
- 1 1/2 c corn flour
- 3 T sugar
- 1 1/2 T baking powder
- 2 t salt
- 1 t cayenne
- 1 1/2 t black pepper
- 2 eggs
- 1/4 c vegetable oil
- 1 1/2 c buttermilk
- 1/4 c diced red pepper
- 1/4 c diced green pepper
- 1/4 c diced onion

In a mixing bowl stir together the dry ingredients—flour, corn flour, sugar, baking powder, salt, cayenne and black pepper.

In a different bowl beat the eggs. Add the oil and buttermilk and beat again. Add the diced vegetables and stir. Add the dry ingredients to the wet, cup by cup, stirring after each addition. Do not overbeat.

Spoon or pour the batter into well oiled or papered muffin tins. Bake for about 20 minutes. These golden crusty spicy muffins are very good with seafoods and sauces.

Carrot Cake

Shena Waugh Sandler

Preheat oven to 350°
Makes a 9" x 13" pan
or 2 9" layers

1/2 c vegetable oil
1 1/3 c sugar
4 eggs
2 1/2 c grated carrots
1 c pineapple pieces
1 c chopped pecans
1 t salt
1 t baking soda
2 T cinnamon
2 c unbleached flour

Cream the oil and the sugar. Add the eggs, one at a time, and then cream together well. Stir in the carrots, the pineapple and the pecans.

Sift together the dry ingredients in a separate bowl, and stir into the batter, one cup at a time.

Pour the batter into oiled and papered pans. Bake about 40 minutes or until the center bounces back to a gentle touch.

The Queen of the Jungle says that macadamia nuts are a good substitute for pecans, and that pineapple is optional.

Devil's Food Cake

Barbara Sanford Smith

Preheat oven to 350°
Makes 2 9" layers

1/2 c water
3 oz unsweetened chocolate
1/2 c butter
3/4 c sugar
1/2 c brown sugar
2 eggs
1 t vanilla extract
2/3 c buttermilk
1/2 t salt
1 t baking soda
2 c unbleached flour

In a small saucepan melt the chocolate in the water. Use a low heat and be careful not to scorch the chocolate. Cream the butter, sugars and eggs together until they are light. Stir in the vanilla and the chocolate mixture.

Sift, then measure the flour. Blend the salt and the baking soda into the flour. Alternately add the dry ingredients and the buttermilk to the batter, stirring after each addition. Pour the batter into the layer pans which have been lined with paper and oiled. Bake approximately 35 minutes or until the layers bounce back after a soft touch to the centers. This cake becomes dry and crumbly if baked too long.

Ebony Cake

Robert Schwartz

Preheat oven to 350°
Makes 2 8" layers

3/4 c butter
1 1/4 c sugar
3 oz unsweetened chocolate
3 eggs
1 1/2 t vanilla extract
1/4 t almond extract
1 1/2 c unbleached flour
1 1/2 c ground walnuts
1 T baking powder
1/2 t salt
3/8 c dark rum
3/8 c strong coffee
3/4 c milk

Cream the butter, then add the sugar and beat well. Add the eggs, one at a time. Beat until light. Melt the chocolate, then add to the mix. Stir in the vanilla and almond extracts.

Sift the flour, then measure into a different bowl. Stir the baking powder and the salt into the flour. Grind the nuts in a blender or food processor. Do not overdo this step or they will become an oily paste. Stir them into the flour mix.

In a large measuring cup, combine the rum, coffee and milk. Add the dry ingredients and the liquids alternately to the batter, stirring after each addition.

Pour the batter into the layer pans which have been papered and oiled, even on top of the papers. Bake for about 35 minutes, until the center tops of the layers bounce back to a soft touch. This cake is very delicate during the baking process. Wait a few minutes after taking from the oven to remove from pans. Wait a few more minutes before removing the papers from the layers.

To assemble this cake, fill with mocha butter cream and cover with chocolate glaze. You may decorate the top with chocolate covered espresso beans.

Fairport Orange Cake

Barbara Sanford Smith

Preheat oven to 350°
Makes 2 9" layers

1 c sugar
1/3 c butter
2 eggs
1 t vanilla extract
2 t orange zest
1/3 c chopped walnuts
1 c buttermilk
1 t baking soda
1/2 t salt
1 3/4 c unbleached flour

This is the easiest cake to make. Combine all the ingredients in a bowl and mix until well blended.

Bake in pans that have been papered and oiled. Baking time is approximately 35 minutes. The layers will pull away from the sides of the pans when done.

German Chocolate

Frederick Becker

Preheat oven to 350°
Makes 2 9" layers

1/2 c water
3 oz unsweetened chocolate
3 oz white chocolate
1/2 c butter
3/4 c sugar
1/2 c brown sugar
2 eggs
1 t vanilla extract
1 t baking soda
1/2 t salt
2 c unbleached flour
2/3 c buttermilk

Filling:
2/3 c cream
2/3 c brown sugar
2 egg yolks
1/3 c butter
1 t vanilla extract
3/4 c coconut
2/3 c pecan pieces

Melt the chocolate in the water in a small saucepan over low heat. Set aside.

Thoroughly cream the butter and the sugars. Add the eggs and the vanilla and beat until light and creamy. Stir in the chocolate mix. In a different bowl, stir the baking soda and the salt into the flour. Alternately add these dry ingredient and the buttermilk to the batter. Beat well.

Pour the batter into the layer pans which have been lined with paper, oiled and lightly floured. Bake for 30 to 35 minutes or until the centers of the layers bounce back to a soft touch.

To make the filling: Cook over a medium heat, stirring occasionally, the cream, brown sugar, butter, egg yolks and vanilla. After they are thick add the coconut and the pecans. Stir until the mixture is gooey. Allow the mixture to cool.

To assemble: Spread the bottom layer of the cake with the filling. Add the top layer and spread that with the remaining filling.

Hundred Dollar Cake

Grandma Degen

Preheat oven to 325°
Makes a 9" x 13" pan
or 2 9" layers

1 c brown sugar
1 c warm water
1 c mayonnaise
1 t vanilla extract
1/4 c cocoa
2 t baking soda
1/2 t salt
2 c unbleached flour

Combine the water and the brown sugar and stir well. Add the mayonnaise and beat well. Stir in the vanilla.

Sift the flour before measuring, then add the cocoa, baking soda, and salt. Add the dry ingredients to the batter a bit at a time, stirring after each addition.

Pour the batter into the pans which have been lined with paper and oiled. Bake for about 40 minutes or until the center of the cake bounces back to a soft touch.

This dark, moist cake keeps well for days.

Mom's Orange Cake

Preheat oven to 350°
Makes 2 9" layers

1/3 c butter
3/4 c sugar
2 eggs, separated
zest of 1 orange
1/4 c orange juice
1/2 t lemon extract
1/2 t vanilla extract
1/4 c milk
2 t baking powder
1 3/4 c unbleached flour

Filling:
1 1/2 c sugar
2/3 c flour
1/2 t salt
4 egg yolks
zest of 2 oranges
3/4 c orange juice
2 T lemon juice

Cream the butter, then add the sugar and the egg yolks. Beat well. Stir in the orange zest, lemon and vanilla extracts.

Sift the flour before measuring into a separate bowl. Add the salt and the baking powder to the flour. Add the flour and the milk alternately to the batter, then the orange juice and the rest of the flour. Beat well.

Whip the egg whites until they are stiff. Fold them into the batter.

Bake in pans which have been lined with paper and oiled. Baking time is about 30 minutes. The center of the layers will bounce back after a soft touch when they are done. After the layers have cooled, split horizontally, spread with orange filling and stack. Mom would frost with a cooked frosting.

To make the filling: In a saucepan mix the sugar, flour and salt. Stir in the beaten egg yolks and the orange zest. Gradually stir in the orange juice and the lemon juice. Cook while stirring over a low heat until the mixture thickens. Cool before adding to the cake layers.

Poppy Seed Cake

The Irenean Hostage

Preheat oven to 350°
Makes 2 9" layers
or a tube pan

1 1/2 c sugar
1 1/2 c butter
3 eggs
1 1/2 c milk
1 1/2 t vanilla extract
3 c unbleached flour
1 T baking powder
1/4 t salt

Thoroughly cream the butter and sugar. Add the eggs, one at a time, stirring in, then beat well until the batter becomes light and fluffy. Add the vanilla and stir.

Sift the flour, then measure into a separate bowl. Add the baking powder, salt and the poppy seeds to the flour. Add the dry ingredients and the milk alternately to the batter, then beat well.

Pour the batter into 2 layer pans which have been lined with paper and oiled or a tube pan which has been oiled and then dusted with flour. Bake for about 45 minutes or until a toothpick comes out clean from the center. Cool for about ten minutes before removing from the pan(s). Cool on a wire rack.

Pumpkin Cake

Preheat oven to 350°
Makes 2 9" layers

1/3 c butter
3/4 c sugar
3 eggs
1 t vanilla extract
1 c pumpkin
2 c unbleached flour
1/4 t nutmeg
1 t cinnamon
1 t baking soda
1/2 t salt
1 c milk

Thoroughly cream the butter and sugar. Add the eggs, one at a time and stir, then add the vanilla. Beat until light and fluffy. Add the pumpkin and mix until blended.

Sift the flour, then measure into a separate bowl. Stir the nutmeg, cinnamon, salt, and baking soda into the flour. Add the dry ingredients to the batter alternately with the milk. Beat well.

Pour the batter into the layer pans which have been lined with papers and oiled. Bake in the preheated oven for about 35 minutes or until the centers of the layers bounce back after a light touch to the centers.

Sour Cream Pound Cake

Ward Bates

Preheat oven to 300°
Makes 1 10" tube pan

6 eggs, separated
1 c butter
2 1/2 c sugar
1 t vanilla extract
3 c sifted flour
1/4 t salt
1/4 t baking soda
2 c sour cream

Beat the egg whites until stiff. Set aside.

Thoroughly cream the butter and sugar. Add the egg yolks, and mix. Add the vanilla and beat until light and fluffy.

Mix the salt and baking soda into the sifted flour. Add the dry ingredients to the batter alternately with the sour cream. Beat well. Fold in the egg whites.

Pour the batter into a tube pan which has been oiled and dusted with flour. Bake for about 1 hour. Allow to cool before removing from pan.

Strawberry Muffins

Inspiration at Zazou

Preheat oven to 400°
Makes 1 dozen

- 2 eggs
- 3/8 c vegetable oil
- 3/4 c sugar
- 2 1/2 c unbleached flour
- 1 1/2 T baking powder
- 1/2 t salt
- 3/4 c slivered almonds
- 1 1/2 c strawberries

Beat together the eggs, oil and sugar until they are creamy. In a separate bowl mix the baking powder, salt and almonds into the flour. If the nuts are lightly toasted on a dry pan for a few minutes, it will enhance the flavor. This is not necessary, but a suggestion which is well worth the effort.

Enough fresh strawberries need to be washed, hulled and crushed to obtain 1 1/2 cups. If you use frozen sweetened berries, then decrease the sugar by 2 tablespoons.

Add the dry ingredients to the mix alternately with the strawberries. Spoon the batter into oiled or papered muffin cups.

Bake in a preheated oven for about 20 minutes, or until the muffins appear golden and bounce back from a soft touch.

Sweet Potato Muffins

Preheat oven to 400°
Makes 1 dozen

2 eggs
2 c sweet potatoes
2 T vegetable oil
1/2 c sugar
1 t vanilla extract
2/3 c unbleached flour
2 T baking powder
1 t baking soda
1/2 t salt
3/4 t nutmeg
1 1/2 t cinnamon
1/2 c raisins
1/2 c chopped pecans
2/3 c buttermilk

Cook or bake the sweet potatoes until they are soft, then peel, mash and measure them. It's a good way to use leftovers.

Whip the sweet potatoes with the eggs, sugar and the oil. Stir in the vanilla.

Combine the dry ingredients in a separate bowl. Alternately add the dry ingredients and the buttermilk to the batter. Mix thoroughly but do not overbeat.

Spoon the batter into oiled or papered muffin pans. Bake in the preheated oven for about 20 minutes or until the muffins bounce back from a soft touch.

Upside-Down Cake

Preheat oven to 325°
Makes a 9" cake

Slices of pineapple
or other fruits
3/4 c brown sugar
1/4 c melted butter
2 eggs, separated
2/3 c sugar
1/2 c fruit juice
1 1/2 c unbleached flour
1/4 t salt
1 t baking powder

whipped cream

When you preheat the oven, place a shallow pan of hot water on the bottom oven rack. Paper and lightly oil a round 9" pan.

Arrange the fruit in the pan with the more attractive side down. Spread the brown sugar over the fruit and drizzle the butter over the sugar.

Separate the eggs. Beat the whites until they are stiff. Set aside.

Mix together the egg yolks and the sugar. Stir in the fruit juice and beat well. Blend the salt and the baking powder into the flour. Stir the dry ingredients into the batter.

Give the egg whites a stir to make sure they are still stiff. Beat again until stiff, if you need to do so. Fold the egg whites into the batter.

Pour the batter evenly over the ingredients already in the pan. Baking time will be about 45 minutes. Wait until the cake is cooled before inverting on a serving platter. Remove the paper carefully. Serve with whipped cream.

White Chocolate Cake

Inspiration at Magazine Cuisine

Preheat oven to 350°
Makes 2 9" layers

1/4 c water
3 oz white chocolate
1/2 c butter
1/2 c sugar
2 eggs
1 t vanilla extract
1 T clear creme de cacao
2 c unbleached flour
1/2 t salt
1 t baking soda
2/3 c milk

Place the water and the chocolate in a small saucepan and melt over low heat, stirring frequently. Set aside.

Thoroughly cream the butter and sugar. Add the eggs and beat until light. Add the vanilla and the creme de cacao and stir. Add the chocolate mix and stir.

Sift the flour and measure into a separate bowl. Add the baking soda and the salt and stir. Add the dry ingredients to the batter alternately with the milk. Beat well.

Pour the batter into the layer pans which have been lined with paper and oiled. Bake for about 35 minutes or until a tooth pick comes out clean from the center of the layers.

PIES & TARTS

Armadillos' Ecstasies

Madeleine McCarthy

Fills 1 dozen tarts

16 oz cream cheese
1 medium banana
1 medium ripe avocado
1 T honey
1 T lemon juice

Toasted cashew pieces

Whip the cream cheese until light and smooth. Add the banana and the avocado and whip until light and smooth. Next, drizzle in the honey and add the lemon juice, and stir in gently.

Make tart shells from a Basic Pastry crust. cut the rolled pastry into squares, fold gently into muffin pans and bake until golden.

Fill the pre-baked tart shells and sprinkle the top with the toasted cashews. Refrigerate until set.

Armadillos have been known to walk all the way from Texas for one of these treats.

Banana Cream Pie

Melinda J. Gleason

Makes 1 9" pie

1/2 c sugar
4 T cornstarch
1/2 t salt
2 c milk
3 egg yolks
3 T butter
2 t vanilla extract
3 egg whites
1/3 c sugar

2 or 3 bananas
1 c whipping cream
2 T powdered sugar
1/2 t vanilla extract

1 baked 9" pie shell

Have the pie shell ready before you make the filling.

In a stainless steel bowl combine the 1/2 cup sugar, cornstarch and salt. Gradually whisk in the milk, then the egg yolks. Cook until thickened over a boiling pot of water.

Remove from the heat before adding the butter and the vanilla. Stir in the butter after it has melted but do not stir as the mix cools or the filling will be runny. Cool to room temperature and then refrigerate.

Beat the egg whites with the 1/3 c sugar until they form stiff, shiny peaks. Fold the egg whites gently into the custard.

Layer the sliced bananas and the custard into the pie shell. Top with sweetened, flavored whipped cream. Refrigerate until serving.

Basic Pastry

Makes a 9" double crust

2 c unbleached flour
1 t salt
1 T sugar
3/4 c butter, shortening or lard
5 to 7 T ice water

There are so many variations that it is good to read the whole recipe before progressing.

The less pastry is handled, the more tender it will be.

Different kinds of fats produce different results. Butter creates the best flavor. Lard makes crust tender. Hydrogenated vegetable shortening produces a consistent result. Many people use it all the time in everything, but for some reason I do not trust the process that hydrogenates oils. Vegetable oil is used by most vegetarians.

I have added a tablespoon of sugar to the crust recipe given as it helps in browning. If I were making a savory quiche, I would leave that out. I might add some herb like basil or oregano or sage or nutmeg.

Measure the dry ingredients into a bowl. Mix with a couple of forks. Using a pastry blender or a fork, cut in the oil product until the mixture looks grainy. The water needs to be extremely cold. Add to the mixture a couple spoonfuls at a time. Toss with two forks to stir. Touch the mixture with your hands as little as possible. Only add as much water as it takes to have the dough stick together.

If you wrap the dough in plastic wrap and refrigerate for a while, it will roll more easily. You may roll on a pastry cloth, waxed paper or a counter dusted lightly with flour. Handle very delicately.

Pie shells may be stored in the freezer and baked later. Preheat oven to 400°. Bake for 10 minutes at that temperature, then reduce heat to 350° and bake until golden or until the center of a fruit pie boils.

Buttermilk Custard Pie

Ira Long, Jr.

Preheat oven to 375°
Makes 1 9" pie

2 T butter
1 3/4 c sugar
4 eggs
2 t vanilla extract
1 pinch nutmeg
4 T flour
1/2 t baking powder
1/2 t baking soda
2 c buttermilk

Cream the softened butter with the sugar. Add the eggs and beat well. Add the vanilla, nutmeg, flour, and baking powder and stir. With a fork stir the baking soda into the buttermilk, then stir this into the batter. Pour into an uncooked pie shell. Sprinkle the top with freshly grated nutmeg.

Bake at 375° for ten minutes, then reduce the heat to 300° and bake until set in the center, about 40 minutes.

Chocolate Cream Tarts

Anne E. Degen Hernandez

Fills 1 dozen tarts

1 1/2 c whipped cream
3 T cocoa
6 T powdered sugar

miniature chocolate chips

Whip the cream until it forms soft peaks. Sift in the cocoa and the powdered sugar. Whip just long enough to incorporate the additional ingredients. Mound into baked tart shells and top with tiny chocolate chips.

Chocolate Pecan Bourbon Pie

Esther Carpenter

Preheat oven to 400°
Makes 1 9" pie

4 eggs
3 T melted butter
1/3 c sugar
2/3 c brown sugar
1/3 c corn syrup
3 T maple syrup
1 oz bourbon
1 t vanilla extract
1 c pecan halves
2/3 c chocolate chips

1 raw pie shell

Beat the eggs. Pour in the melted butter, and beat until well blended. Add the sugars and blend until all of the lumps disappear. Stir in the corn syrup, maple syrup and the vanilla.

Set this mixture aside for a few minutes while you line the bottom of the uncooked pie shell with the chocolate chips. Pour in the filling mixture. Place the pecan pieces to cover the top of the pie.

Place the pie in the oven, close the door and immediately lower the oven temperature to 275°. Cooking time is at least 30 minutes. When the filling is set to the center, the pie is done.

Cranberry Apple Pie

Preheat oven to 400°
Makes 1 9" pie

2 c raw cranberries
1/2 c water
2 c sliced apples
1 c sugar
1 t cinnamon
4 T cornstarch
1 t vanilla extract

1 uncooked pie shell
pastry–lattice or
leaf top
cinnamon sugar

Cook the cranberries with the water in a covered saucepan until the skins pop. Add the sliced apples, stir, and cook for a couple minutes more. Remove from the heat. Stir in the vanilla.

Mix together the sugar, cinnamon and cornstarch. Stir these into the fruit filling. Pour the filling into the pie shell. On top of the filling place lattice strips or pastry cut into leaf shapes with a cookie cutter. Sprinkle the top with cinnamon sugar.

Bake in the 400° oven for 10 minutes. Reduce the oven temperature to 350° and bake until the pie bubbles to the center.

Fruit Pies

Preheat oven to 425°

4 to 5 c fruit
1 to 1 1/2 c sugar or brown sugar
6 T flour or cornstarch
spices and flavorings

1 uncooked pie shell

imagination

The important parts are the fruit, sweetening, thickening, and the flavorings. For the fruit you may use apples, apricots, cherries, nectarines, peaches, rhubarb, berries of any kind, or a mixture of any of these that sounds good to you.

It is likely that sour fruits need more sweetener than sweet fruits. You may use either kind of sugar, a combination of both, or honey.

Regarding the choice of flavorings, it is good to be subtle and let the flavor of the fruit come through. Cinnamon and sometimes a bit of nutmeg or ground cloves are good. Sometimes you may want a little vanilla extract or a tiny bit of almond extract. Lemon juice can add a little zing.

The look of a pie can vary. My mom, who is a great pie maker, uses a solid top with a design of air holes for apples, but a lattice top for colorful berries. I like to use cookie cutters and place one leaf on each piece. Brushing the crust with milk or egg wash create different looks. Sprinkling the top with cinnamon sugar is sometimes nice.

Preheat the oven to 425°. This initial high temperature bakes the bottom crust so it doesn't get soggy. After about 10 minutes reduce the oven temperature to 350°. Bake for about an hour, until the pie boils to the center. It's a good idea to put a piece of aluminum foil or a tray under you pie to catch drips. Good pies always boil over and it's not so much fun to clean the oven.

Graham Cracker Crust

Preheat oven to 350°
Makes 1 9" shell

- 2 c graham cracker crumbs
- 1/2 c unbleached flour
- 2/3 c sugar
- 1 t cinnamon
- 1/2 c melted butter

Mix together all of the dry ingredients in a bowl. Melt the butter over a low heat in a small pan. Drizzle the melted butter over the dry ingredients and toss together with two forks. Press into a pie pan.

Bake for about 20 minutes in the preheated oven.

Key Lime Pie

Jon Kronenberg

Makes 1 9" pie

- 1 envelope unflavored gelatin
- 1/4 c water
- 1/2 c sugar
- 1/4 t salt
- 1/2 c lime juice
- 4 eggs separated
- 1/4 c sugar

- 1 c whipping cream
- 2 T powdered sugar

- pie shell or graham cracker crust

Dissolve the gelatin in the water and set aside. Measure the 1/2 cup sugar and the salt into a saucepan. Stir in the lime juice. Stir in the egg yolks which have been beaten with a fork. Cook this mixture until thick, stirring constantly. Remove from the heat and stir in the gelatin mix. Set aside to cool to room temperature.

Whip the egg whites with the 1/4 c sugar until it forms shiny, stiff peaks. Fold the whites into the cooled lime mixture. Carefully transfer to the chilled prepared pie shell. Top with the whipped, sweetened cream and refrigerate until serving.

Lemon Meringue Pie

Makes 1 9" pie

Filling:
1/4 c lemon juice
1 t lemon zest
1/2 c sugar
3 T cornstarch
1/4 t salt
1 c water
3 egg yolks

Meringue:
3 egg whites
1/8 t cream of tartar
2 T sugar

1 baked pie shell

Prepare the lemon juice and the zest.

In a stainless steel bowl combine the sugar, cornstarch and the salt. Add the water and whisk until smooth. Add the egg yolks and whisk again. Cook this over a saucepan of boiling water, stirring occasionally. After this mix has become thick, remove from the heat and add the butter, lemon juice and zest. After the butter has melted, stir in. Pour into the pie shell and refrigerate until thoroughly chilled.

Before starting to make the meringue, turn on the oven to broil. Beat the egg whites with the cream of tartar and the sugar until shiny, stiff peaks form. Cover the top of the pie with the meringue using a spatula or a pastry tube. Place in the oven under the broiler for just a few minutes until the tips of the meringue peaks brown. Return to the refrigerator until serving.

Peach Daiquiri Pie

Inspiration in New Orleans

Makes 1 9" pie

1 T unflavored gelatin
1/4 c water
4 eggs, separated
1/2 c sugar
3 T cornstarch
2 T fresh lime juice
3 c fresh peaches, pureed
1/4 c rum

baked pie shell
whipped cream
8 slices lime

Dissolve the gelatin in the water and set aside. Beat the egg whites with 1/4 cup sugar until they form shiny, stiff peaks. Set aside.

Stir the remaining sugar in a saucepan with the cornstarch. Add the egg yolks and stir until smooth. Add the pureed peaches and the lime juice. Place over a low heat and stir constantly until thickened. Remove from heat and stir in the gelatin mix and the rum. Cool to room temperature. Fold in the egg whites.

Gently transfer to a pie shell. Garnish each piece with whipped cream and a slice of lime. Refrigerate until serving.

Peanut Butter Pie

Bake shell at 375°
Makes 1 9" pie

Crust:
3 T vegetable oil
1/4 c peanut butter
3/4 c sugar
1 egg yolk
1/2 t vanilla extract
1/2 t baking powder
1 c unbleached flour

Filling:
4 eggs, separated
4 T sugar
4 T cornstarch
2 1/2 c cream
1/2 c peanut butter
1 T vanilla extract

whipped cream
semi-sweet chocolate shavings

To make the crust: Thoroughly cream the oil, peanut butter, sugar, egg yolk and vanilla. Stir the baking powder into the flour. Add the dry ingredients to the wet mix and blend thoroughly. Wrap and chill the dough for at least 30 minutes. Press the dough into the pie pan. Score with several fork marks in the bottom. Bake for about 10 minutes or until golden. Allow to cool before filling.

To make the filling: Beat the egg whites with the sugar until they form soft, shiny peaks. Set aside.

In a saucepan, combine the sugar and the cornstarch. Add enough of the cream to make a smooth mixture. Stir in the egg yolks until evenly blended. Stir in the peanut butter until smooth, then add the rest of the cream and the vanilla. Cook this mixture, stirring constantly until thick. Remove from the heat. Allow to cool before folding in the egg whites.

To assemble: Cover the bottom of the pie shell with chocolate shavings. Add the filling. Sprinkle the top of the filling with more chocolate shavings. Using a star pastry tip, pipe the whipped cream over the pie. Sprinkle with even more chocolate shavings. Chill before serving.

Pecan Pie

Preheat oven to 400°
Makes 1 9" pie

4 eggs
3 T melted butter
3/4 c brown sugar
1 t vanilla extract
1 1/2 c light corn syrup
1 c pecan pieces

1 uncooked pie shell

Beat the eggs. Pour in the melted butter and continue beating until the color is noticeably lighter. Sprinkle in the brown sugar and beat again. Add the vanilla and the corn syrup. Blend until smooth. Pour into the pie shell. Cover the top with pecans.

Bake at 400° for ten minutes. Lower the oven temperature to 350° and bake until set in the center, approximately 25 minutes more.

Pumpkin Pie

Preheat oven to 400°
Makes 1 9" pie

1 1/2 c pumpkin
2/3 c brown sugar
1 t cinnamon
1/2 t ginger
1/2 t nutmeg
3 eggs
1 c whipping cream
1/2 c bourbon
3 T pecan pieces

1 9" uncooked pie shell

Blend the pumpkin with the brown sugar, spices and eggs. Fresh pumpkin tastes much better than canned. Stir in the bourbon. Whip the cream until lightly peaked. Fold into the pumpkin mix. Carefully transfer to the pie shell. Sprinkle the pecan pieces in a ring around the outside edge of the pie.

Bake at 400° for ten minutes, then about 25 minutes more at 350° until the pie is set to the center.

Strawberry Rhubarb Tarts

Makes 1 dozen

4 c fresh rhubarb
2/3 c water
3/4 c sugar
3 T cornstarch
1 t vanilla extract
2 c sliced fresh strawberries

baked tart shells
whipped cream

Wash the rhubarb and cut into 1 inch pieces. Place in a saucepan with the water, cover and cook until softened. Measure the sugar and stir the corn starch into it. Pour this into the cooked rhubarb. Stir until the dry ingredients are mixed evenly. Return to the stove and cook while stirring until the mixture has thickened. Remove from the heat. Stir in the strawberries which have been washed and sliced. Fill the baked tart shells with the filling and refrigerate until served. You may want to garnish the tarts with whipped cream.

Sweet Potato Pie

Preheat oven to 400°
Makes 1 9" pie

1 1/2 c cooked sweet potatoes
3 eggs
1 c heavy cream
3/4 c brown sugar
1 t cinnamon
1/2 t nutmeg
1 t vanilla extract
1 T rum

1 uncooked pie shell
whipped cream
toasted pecans

Whip the sweet potatoes until smooth and creamy. Add the eggs and beat until light. Add the brown sugar and beat until all the lumps are gone. Add the cream and blend until evenly mixed. Stir in the spices, the vanilla and the rum.

Pour the filling into the pie shell. Bake in a 400° oven for ten minutes, then reduce the heat to 325°. Continue to bake until puffy and golden and set to the center, about 25 minutes more. Remove from the oven and cool.

Before serving top with whipped cream and a few toasted pecans.

FROSTINGS, GLAZES, ICINGS & SAUCES

Brandy Orange Icing

1/3 c butter
1/4 c cream cheese
3 T brandy
3 T orange juice
1 T grated orange zest

Whip together the butter and the cream cheese. Add the brandy and the orange juice and zest. Add the powdered sugar gradually until it is a spreadable consistency.

Chocolate Frosting

2/3 c melted butter
2/3 c cocoa
2/3 c milk
2 t vanilla extract
5 c powdered sugar

Mix the vanilla and the cocoa into the melted butter. Add the milk and the first couple cups of powdered sugar. Stir carefully. Keep adding sugar until a spreadable consistency is achieved.

Chocolate Glaze

1 c semi-sweet chocolate chips
3 T dark rum
3/4 c unsalted butter

Melt the chocolate in the rum, being careful not to scorch it. Stir in the butter, one spoonful at a time. Beat over a pan of cold water until spreading consistency.

Cognac Sauce

2 lb seedless grapes
1 c water
1/2 c honey
1 c sugar
juice of 1 lemon
1/4 c cognac

Wash the grapes and remove all of the stems. Mash the grapes or puree in a blender, leaving them rustically lumpy. Combine all of the ingredients, except the cognac in a sauce pan and cook over low flame until syrupy. Remove from heat and stir in the cognac. Good with any cheese cake.

Cream Cheese Icing

1/2 c butter
8 oz cream cheese
1 T vanilla extract
1/2 t lemon juice
4 c powdered sugar

Beat the butter and the cream cheese together until they are soft and smooth. Add the vanilla and lemon juice and stir in. Add the powdered sugar, cup by cup, until a spreadable consistency is achieved.

Danish Glaze

3/4 c water
1 T lemon juice
1 t vanilla extract
2 c powdered sugar

Stir the liquids together and add the sugar a bit at a time until thin and brushable.

Glaze for Apple Bread

1/4 c milk
1 t vanilla extract
2 c powdered sugar

Beat together until smooth. Will be brushable.

Glaze for Lemon Bread

4 T Lemon juice
1 c powdered sugar

Beat until smooth. Needs to be thin for brushing.

Lebkuchen Glaze

3 T hot water
1/2 t lemon extract
1 t lemon juice
1 1/2 c powdered sugar

Stir all of the liquids together. Add the powdered sugar a bit at a time, stirring out all lumps. This will be a brushable consistency.

Mocha Butter Cream

1 c butter
4 T strong coffee
2 c powdered sugar

Whip the butter until light and creamy. Add the coffee and the powdered sugar at the same time, beat until smooth.

Orange Frosting

6 T butter
juice of 1 orange
zest of 1 orange
3 c powdered sugar

Whip the butter until soft. Add all other ingredients and beat until it is a smooth spreadable consistency.

Raspberry Icing

(For your Valentines)

- 1/4 c raspberry juice
- 1/4 c butter
- 1 c powdered sugar

Whip the butter until light. Add the juice and sugar at the same time. Beat until smooth and brushable.

Rum Sauce

- 3/4 c brown sugar
- 1/4 c honey
- 6 T butter
- 2 T rum
- 1 T Gran Marnier
- 1 t vanilla extract

Heat the butter, brown sugar and honey in a saucepan over medium flame. Stir constantly until they are almost boiling. Remove from the heat and whisk in the rum and vanilla. Serve hot over bread pudding or the dessert of your choice.

Sweet E. Bun Glaze

- 8 oz cream cheese
- 2/3 c honey
- 1/2 t vanilla extract

Cream the cream cheese until soft and smooth. Gradually add the honey, making sure you scrape down the sides of the bowl and the mixture has no lumps. Stir in the vanilla.

Index